A TREE ELVES'

Christmas

COCKTAIL BOOK

CMB

a MIXOLOGIST'S COMPENDIUM of SEASONAL SPIRITS and much MERRY-MAKING

AUTHORED BY André duBignon Furin

FEATURING ILLUSTRATIONS BY

Adèle Newton Furin

APPRECIATIONS

I APPRECIATE NICK AND STEVEN CARSE
AND THE KING OF POPS for allowing me to launch the
Royal College of Inspiration and the Potions & Alchemy course
in 2017, as well as offering me their warm encouragement to
pursue this specific project in conjunction with the Tree Elves'
season, without which it would not have been so soon in coming.

I APPRECIATE MY MOM'S BOUNDLESS LOVE, her belief
in my passionate endeavors, and her freely sharing her illustra-
tive talent with me (especially when I kinda expect her to read my
mind based off a few broadstroke directives and just "go for it").

I APPRECIATE THE AMAZING GRAPHIC DESIGNER who
accepted this task after our enjoyable work together on Book 1 of
Legends from the Dragon Scribe in 2014. Dot Dodd challenges
me in all the perfect ways and propels my work to much greater
standards. Much of what you find within is a product of that magic.

I APPRECIATE THE GREAT MIXOLOGISTS WHO CAME
BEFORE US. Those who craft the spirits with recipes as old as
centuries and those who curate them into a special gift to taste.
Thank you.

I APPRECIATE YOU, THE READER — the current generation
mixologist, who will be working with the recipes herein, and
improving upon them in your own special ways. Cheers!

FINALLY, I APPRECIATE THE MANY MANY DEAR
FRIENDS who have accompanied me on this magical
journey of discovery and revelation. I love you!
Merry MERRY Christmas!!!

BROUGHT TO YOU BY:

TREE ✦ ELVES
A KING OF POPS COMPANY

Publisher's Cataloging-in-Publication data

LIBRARY of CONGRESS CONTROL NUMBER

Furin, André duBignon
Illustrations by Adèle Newton Furin

ISBN-13: 978-0-9960554-5-1

Filament Eleven Press
Design and Layout by Dot Dodd

PRINTED IN THE UNITED STATES OF AMERICA

Third Paperback November 2021
12 11 10 9 8 7 6 5 4 3

CONTENTS

FOREWORD

In 2010, my brother, Nick, and I started a company that sold ice pops out of a push cart on a street corner in Atlanta. We named our business King of Pops. Our fledgling operation was a little rough around the edges, but it was also interesting and good hearted. It took off - growing more quickly than anyone would have guessed.

As our team expanded, the slower pop sales in the winter became a larger strain, and we were looking for ways to flatten our businesses seasonality. We were already a jolly bunch, so we decided to start a Christmas Tree delivery business called Tree Elves. So now each holiday season, we don our elf outfits and create Christmas memories for thousands of families across the South.

We've seen first hand that life is better when we put ourselves out there. André did this selflessly when she started this project.

Her book will be a success if you pick one of these recipes (or go off script) and mix up a drink that you might not have shared with someone otherwise. Put yourself out there this year - I promise you won't be disappointed.

–Steven Carse
"CHIMNEY" THE TREE ELF
CO-FOUNDER OF KING OF POPS

Some of my most fond memories of Christmastime involve Christmas Trees, oversized elves, and an occasional cocktail to celebrate. This compendium brings all of that emotion together in a way that anyone can mix up a toddy or nog and share it with loved ones during the most spirited season of the year!

–Nick Carse
"TINSEL" THE TREE ELF
CO-FOUNDER OF KING OF POPS

INTRODUCTION

INTRODUCTION

In my mid-twenties I discovered the 1961 edition of Old Mr. Boston that my father kept in his black and white checkerboard-tiled bar. I was fascinated by it, as if it were a mysterious book that held the alchemical formulae for the Elixir of Life. During the holidays—after everyone went to sleep in the house and I stayed watch over a crackling hearth fire—I would return to the worn red-covered book and its hundreds of random illustrations.

The book was given to my father by a friend of his during their early twenties, that friend-for-life, "Rog Thaler," would become the best man in my parents' wedding over 50 years ago. Little does he know what a treasure he bestowed upon my father, my siblings, and me. For this simple gift was and is the inspiration for this Christmas Cocktail Book.

It is my belief that sharing and building upon such classic recipes is a marvelous way of honoring the magnificent heritage and possibilities of our current cocktail culture *and* of forging a rich network among those of us in this modern era aspiring to elevate life throughout these dark winter months and enliven our own LIFE stories. The remarkably elaborate and complex history of spirits and their accompaniments (liqueurs, brandies, bitters, syrups, shrubs, wines and so-on-and-so-forth) have become an elegant means of bottling the present moment as a product for future generations. To me, this is a remarkable gift.

I have included a robust appendix denoting the origin of all the recipes included herewithin, both for reference and as a source to which you will turn to deepen your own appreciation of mixology, cocktails, and their multi-faceted legends of origin. This bibliography, of sorts, can be found towards the end of this book.

In a way, aged liqueurs and fortified wines become all the more special when paired together in unique libations to share, taste, and savor with our beloveds. These treasured recipes are included in hopes that they inspire you, your family, and your friends. May you please honor, respect, and value them — these wondrous gifts that our modern era has received from the graciousness of our predecessors. In addition, many of the mixologists whose recipes are included in this book own fabulous bars today. Please visit them, purchase their own books and their own cocktails at the source, and heap the appropriate laudations upon them! It will do us all good.

– ANDRÉ DUBIGNON FURIN
Professor of Potions & Alchemy at the Royal College of Inspiration

As a final note (of this introduction), my intent is to publish this Christmas Cocktail Book annually and to improve upon it as the spirit of Christmas matures within me year-over-year.

Therefore, if you have a cocktail, Christmas story, or sidebar item (etc.) that you wish for me to include, please send your comments:

BY POST:
P.O. Box 54846; Atlanta, GA 30308

or BY EMAIL.
ChristmasCocktailBook@gmail.com

To order additional copies of this title, visit:
https://tinyurl.com/y3b2nj4q

ADVENT
PAGES

Below you will find several pages packed with daily meditations to muse upon as you prepare for Thanksgiving, throughout Advent, through the Golden Days of Christmas, past the threshold of the Old and New Years, and towards the Epiphany.

I've included these emergent items as context and as inspiration for the Spirit of Christmas, with which I approach the decorum of the craft cocktail. My hope is that by including them, you will be inspired to bring Christmas into your hearts and upon your hearth, AND that your toasts will become overflowing with merriment and excellent cheer, as they will surely issue forth from a space of great wealth: the joy within your own heart!

———— ◇ ————

warm ciders, mulled with spice —
and eggnog with good (Four Roses)
Bourbon, Manhattans and Old
Fashions, for the love of
New York City

beeswax tapers

medicinal elixirs (joyful and peaceful)
to thoroughly heal oneself and one
another

good fortune

expressions of the myriad
manifestations of love

celebration, letting our hearts
sing, cause for Joy, depth and
completeness of breath

Light in our Hearts and our homes

sharing, giving, being courteous,
kindness, and radiating peace

radical anti-establishment
revolutionary, as by the ways and
means of Peace

thoughtful, gratitude, sharing love,

gifts, welcome: stories

tapered candles & candelabra

the pink candle = Joy. (3 purple, 1
pink): lit each Sunday (1st Sunday is
December 2nd)

— differs from an "advent calendar"

which always begins same date:
December 1st.

A time of light in our hearts when
we are increasingly experiencing
darkness. It is coming together
to sing and make-merry and
CELEBRATE all of the gifts we
have received throughout the year,
and have merged with our own
ability to share light. Opportunity
to revisit Light 4 times, with
quadruplicate awareness.

Holly green, ivy green, winter green,
warmth, sharing warmth, crackling
fires, hot cider, hot beverages, tea,
joviality, the best within each of us:
the smells of the kitchen, the smell

of the evergreen trees.

Fraser Fir, wreath, garland; the smell is heavenly, glorious, uplifting, sensational, joyful, rejuvenating, exciting.

Being in the bar and kitchen mixing up drinks —crafting and nourishing our beloveds; outpouring of love. Nativity, and infinite, unfathomable, replenishable, abundant hope. Song from our cores.

Relationships to one another, being courteous and kind, radiant peace, acts of Thanksgiving.

Tenderness and thoughtfulness.our ability to perform miracles by our love. Story-telling.

The Holy Spirit, Bethlehem, shepherds, night watch, flock, angel(s) of the Lord, "Do not be afraid," "great joy," the city of David, lying in a manger, "and Mary kept all these things, reflecting on them in her heart." "a pair of turtledoves," "so that the thoughts of many hearts may be revealed," "the light shines in the darkness, and the darkness has not overcome it." 14+14+14 = 42 generations of patience; "magi from the east;" "the star's appearance," "Then they opened their treasures and offered him gifts of gold, frankincense, and myrrh." following the Right way. dreams.

expressing gratitude tangibly,

wrapping to good music and good vibes. Incense, memories of our own childhoods, playfulness, coziness, [story-laden] ornaments, the Christmas tree, lights on the tree, watering the tree, lights, lights, lights, reindeer hooves, elves, Santa's workshop (a carpenter!), Santa's sleigh, red, green, white, love, furry, fuzzy, warm, cozy, snuggles, hugs, closeness, familiarity, crisp air, crackers, generosity, Mass, Christmas cheer, openness, calm, quiet, hush of snow, children sleeping, children playing, excitement, building up, David, adventures, quiet streets, Christmas morning.

Tree Elf season

the winter solstice (Friday December 21st, 2018)

The Holy Family

L'ésprit de Noël, the Sugar Plum Fairy, the goat shed, "Bonjour!" (chevre)

Ring (bells ring); the smell of sap, resin of needles, chimneys, warmth, cookies, milk, merriment, good cheer, symphony orchestra, boys' choirs, Visions, records, soups, popcorn, stockings, Grandmother's recipes, peppermint ice cream, peppermint chocolate, visits, long visits, relaxed visits, games, game nights, A Christmas Carol - read aloud.

old classics (movies, film)¡ greenery, charming, delightful, warm/ bright pockets when surrounded by cold/ darkness, mittens, warm house-socks, sitting by a crackling and popping open fire, logs, yule logs, mistletoe, cabins, woods, nobility, hope, Christmas tree lots, Macy's Cellar, chocolates, Rich's Christmas tree, the Pink Pig, Snowflake Lane, choir, bells, the treehouse, the kneeling Santa at the manger with his hat off, Krampus.

being surprised by someone else's thoughtfulness, deep desires being [secretly] acknowledged and met. anticipating deepest and unspoken wants. pre-planning, meaningful gifts, consideration, a month (4 weeks/ 24 days) of preparation¡ gentleness, kinship, kindred spirits, the Christmas Elf, outside, fresh air, books, reading, abundance, resourcefulness, craftiness, sharing music, sharing life experiences, forgiveness, gaiety, merriment, good cheer, frisbees

The Christmas Spirit

thorough breaths, exercise in crisp, cold air, blue skies and white and evergreen, travels by Donkey, travels by Camels, riches, the Nativity scene, Joseph, Star of Bethlehem, Christmas Day, Christmas Eve, preparations, cheerfulness, helpfulness, togetherness, festive, panettone,

confidence, confiding, wishing, speaking secrets of the heart aloud, making dreams come true, heart-happiness, peace, tranquility, Joy, the love for children.

French horns, trumpets, jubilation, deliciousness, sleeping bags, planning, stealthiness, skiing, Christmas gifts, presents, presence, rich in spirit, appreciation, gratitude, travels, MAGIC, Miracles, gathering festivities, massage, relaxation, breath, tenderness, thoughtfulness, socks, fireplace, cooking, new recipes, adventure.

Truth. the hay (the food of the goats), not the straw (their bedding) is softer¡ hence the manger.

True Stories.

Christmas cards, Christmas letters, hibernation, ribbons, bows, manifesting appreciation, end-of-term, end-of-quarter, end-of-year, wrapping things up. macaroons, prayer for peace, peace in our hearts.

warm welcome. ballet, mistletoe, holding hands, cappuccino, markets, dark greens, exploration/ tastes, senses, simplicity, ease.

newness of many things.

Midnight Mass, long hot baths, long showers, sleeping, dreaming, imagination, romanticism, whipping cream, early mornings, dark at daybreak, stars, sweaters, winter's fog, trains, steam, long books, book series, surprises, kindness, friends, dancing, music, nuts.

being generous, being gracious, mutual love & affection; feeling valued; Matriarchs; home; wrapping paper; walkers-by; feasting; new memories; Auld Lang Syne; It's a Wonderful Life; companionship; patience; Otto Luttece.

renew, rebirth, baked meringues, cold moons, dates, new day, new year, imagery, prophecies, voices, monks, Hebrew, Arabic, Latin, Egyptian, Celtic, bells, awakening, awareness, Luke, childhood, nights, purity, doing good, doing well, healing, virtues, values, learning, stories.

compassion, cheerfulness, peacefulness, candlelight, anticipation, fortitude, transformation, communication, St. Nicholas, magic, mystery, secrets, fun, midnight hours, clarity, understanding, brilliance, wonderment, meditation, hearts.

Amazing, Restful, Inspiring

simplicity, being home, yuletide greetings, rosy cheeks, sleigh bells, silver bells, St. Mary, Cathedral, resonance, grace, BEing, deer, elk, bison, wolves, maps, roads, pathways, mix tapes, jolly, "click, click, click," expectancy, arrival, celebration, abundance, leftovers, creation,

endurance, strength, courage,

fortitude, fortify, motherhood, partnerships, relationships, birthplace, routes, journey, righteousness, hospitality, welcomeness, forgiveness, flow, ease, birth, support, gentleman, Joseph, heritage, matrilineal, genealogy, family tree, significance, song, story, embrace, conception, teaching, renewal.

ointment, the Drummer Boy, Pops, Alpine, mountains, hosts, toasts, grandeur, our very best, kindling, kindling wood, tradition, culture, company, wisdom, participation, matrimony, laughter, hands clasped, sincerity, Awe, intentions, self-love, horns, organ, care, returning home, smell of home, reconnection, friendliness, human kindness, On High, guiding lights, reciprocity, contemplation, solitude, rejuvenation, renewal, relaxation, reinvigoration, rebirth, purification, childlike, innocence, gifts, green, white.

gaiety, contemplation, rich, tasty, sensuous, complete, decorations, congenial, neighborly, amicable, toasty, lively, animated, long nights, cold, warm, tales, reading, sharing, amplification, loyalty, dedication, all kinds of love, illumination, hymnals, song books, extravagance, goodness, blessings, exemplars, antiquity, spices, engagement, betrothed, comfort, serenity, togetherness, custom, shared-enthusiasm, fires, Nature, spirit, authenticity, effort, rest, fullness, realizations, moments, passage of time, childhood, adulthood, grandparents, perseverance.

"first footing," Good King Wenceslas, Ding Dong Merrily on High, la grande crême.

glad tidings, gloves, scarves, hats, felt, wool, capilene, layers, vests, undergarments, nightgowns, footie pajamas, robes, endearing, Jesus!, thoughtfulness, anticipation, closeness, Strawberry Shortcake.

hooves, cattle, sheep, lamb of God, sandals, sand, munificence, wood, wooden, blankets, rest, calm.

Single-origin coffees, Virgin, miracles, earnestness, High Holidays, children, wholesomeness, Tree Elves, true love, packages, parcels, St. Nick.

genuine, Believe, good health, talents, purity, breath, firelight, winter sky, The Heavens, Our Story, merriment, Thankfulness, wisdom, metaphors, proverbs, fables, riches, rubies, emeralds, diamonds, graciousness, coming together, stillness, rejoicing, singing, language, culture, mercy, the sun, hearts, growth, maturity, transformation, radical revolution of the ways of PEACE, Love, Light, communion, exaltation, Birth. going Home. traveling.

carriage, rosy cheeks, light of candles

glowing in the church, stained-glass, fond memories, thoughtful consideration, Christmas Mass, choir loft, trust, secrets of our hearts, strength, energy, courage, abundance, Presence, heart-warming, Peace is possible, mortals, excited, joyful, love, Blessings, marvelous, amazing, awesome, goodness of the human spirit, powerful, innocent, pure, Joyous Love, integrity, humility, renewal, healing, virtuous, kind, loving, courteous, betterment, waiting gracefully, maturity, gestation, fascination, Abbey, Feast of St. Stephen, reaching out to the ones we love and letting them know we love them, being open and honest, our shared humanity, staying in touch, feeling connected, letting go of our fears, loving, enjoying the present moment, trusting, suspending judgment, anticipated season, time for hope, significance, our Light, swelling hearts, capacity to love and be loved and be in awe, smiles, greetings, atmosphere, hustle and bustle, good spirit, reunions, yesteryear, pouring out our love, days of yore, forgive, heal, repair, mend, replenish, nourishment, collective peace and joy, dancing close, embraced in love, old and new traditions, reflection, story-telling, time of leisure, replenishment, symphonies, choruses, well-behaved children, our innocence, youthfulness.

Being an instrument of Peace. a
wondrous life! Marvels.

Peace in our hearts.

flourishes, the Patronus Charm

WASSAIL

WASSAIL

To me, Wassail hallmarks the height of the Christmas season and is thus a "recipe" that stands distinct amongst other "cocktails;" hence its place as the forerunner in this book, setting the tone for the winter we wish to intentionally invite into our lives, as we set about giving thanks for the many blessings of the past and setting resolutions towards a better future.

Wassail is a hot mulled beverage (punch, mead, cider, wine, or ale) associated with Yuletide glee and to be served from a "wassailing bowl." Great bowls and their beautifully decorated lids were carved of wood, thrown from pottery, or fashioned from precious metals, such as silver. They became an important and revered vessel with traditional acclaim.

There are many legends of the earliest versions of wassail. However, it seems clear that it began as a warmed mulled mead made with apples and drunk by shepherds, which (by the time of Shakespeare) evolved to become a mulled cider made with sugar, cinnamon, ginger and nutmeg, and served with a ladle from a large communal bowl.

Today's modern recipes might begin with a base of wine, fruit juice or mulled ale, sometimes with brandy, sherry, or other spirits added, in addition to apples or oranges. Really, the choice is yours, as long as your heart rings true, it is warmed, it is shared, and it tastes delicious!

"Wassailing" refers to a traditional ceremony that involves singing and drinking to the health of the [apple] trees on Twelfth Night (eve of January 6th) in the hopes that they might best thrive. The term "wassailing" has become synonymous with "caroling" because carolers (upon finishing their few songs) would be invited into the warm, well-lit, cozy homes of their neighbors to imbibe, catch-up, and share in the good cheer of the season.

As a child, "Here We Come a Wassailing" was among my top favorite Christmas songs to go about singing. It felt like the perfect embodiment of the Christmas spirit: to sing out with merry voices, to welcome one another, and to share in our abundance during the darkest season of the year.

My hope is that by including Wasail as a precursor to this Christmas Cocktail Book, that we, once more, will enliven the traditional activity of going about singing to one another and inviting one another into our homes to celebrate our lives, our collective health, and our well-being.

So, may the songs rise from your hearts and heal your ails, and may you raise your goblets in a communal toast and, together, raise up your voices:

"TO YOUR HEALTH!"

BROADSIDES

(SONGS BY WHICH TO GO A' CAROLING
AND CAROLS WITH WHICH TO WASSAIL)

"GOD REST YOU MERRY, GENTLEMAN"
"I SAW THREE SHIPS"
"THE FIRST NOWELL"
"JOY TO THE WORLD! THE LORD IS COME"
"THE HOLLY AND THE IVY"
"GOOD KING WENCESLAS"
"HERE WE COME A WASSAILING"

TIPS ON HOW TO KINDLY GO A-CAROLING:

- Organize a group of carolers (ideally less than 8 and more than 3)
- Ask permission of houses you wish to visit (and the final house)
- Provide broadsides for all carolers
- Sing only 2-3 songs at each house, unless implored to sing more
- Only stay for 1 small drink (except at the final house)
- Be respectful (time of evening, neighbors, etc.)

TIPS ON HOW TO RECEIVE WARM-HEARTED CAROLERS

- When the doorbell rings or the knock is heard upon the door, invite all those present in the home to crowd around the door and listen to the carolers
- Clap after each song
- After the carolers have finished their singing, invite them in for a small cup of wassail and a piece of toast
- Speak well of their singing and share the good news of the year while you drink to their health

EGG NOGS

AN INTRODUCTION TO EGG NOG

The word "Egg Nog" has many legendary etymological origins. One such purported story is that a "noggin" was the name of the small drinking vessel with an upright handle from which one served this hearty yuletide classic.

There are many many egg nogs, as there are many homes and traditions of Christmas. Here is a sampling of some of our favorites, tried-and-true. Please feel free to send us your own (and the stories that accompany them), and we'll look forward to including them in future editions of this Christmas Cocktail Book!

ON PASTEURIZING YOUR EGGS

Use fresh eggs. As a general rule, relatively fresh eggs are safer to use than old eggs. Do not use an egg that is past its expiration date and never use an egg that has any cracks in the shell. Ideally, you'll use farm fresh, local, free-range, cage-free, organic, yada-yada-yada, "the freshest!" eggs.

Bring the eggs to room temperature. Take the eggs you plan on using out of the refrigerator and let them sit out on your kitchen counter for 15 to 20 minutes. The shell of each egg should feel close to room temperature before you proceed any further.

Do not use chilled eggs for this procedure. The egg yolks need to reach a temperature of 138 degrees before potential bacteria will die, but cold eggs may not warm up sufficiently during the limited amount of time they can spend in the warm water used for pasteurizing. Room temperature eggs, on the other hand, have a better chance.

Place the eggs in a saucepan of water. Fill a small saucepan halfway with cool to cold water. Carefully place the eggs inside the water, laying them on the bottom of the saucepan in a single layer.

If necessary, add more water to the saucepan after placing the eggs inside. The eggs should be covered by about 1" of water.

Attach an instant-read thermometer to the side of the pan. Make sure that the tip of the thermometer rests underneath the water so that it can read the temperature of the water throughout the process. You will need to monitor the temperature very closely.

Note that any instant-read thermometer will work, but a digital thermometer is probably your best bet since it allows you to read temperature fluctuations more precisely.

Slowly heat the water. Place the saucepan on the stove and heat it using a medium heat setting. Allow the water to reach a temperature of 140

Ideally, you should not allow the temperature of the water to rise above 142 degrees during any point of the process. At higher temperatures, the consistency and properties of the egg could be altered. You may end up cooking the eggs slightly without even realizing it.

In a pinch, however, you might be able to allow the temperature to rise as high as 145-150 without seeing significant changes in the quality of the raw egg. In particular, if you are not using a thermometer, you will need to watch the water and wait for bubbles to form on the bottom of the pan. When that happens, the temperature of the water have reached about 150.

Maintain the temperature for three to five minutes. With the water temperature remaining constant temperature, continue heating large eggs for a full three minutes. Extra large eggs should be kept in the hot water for five minutes.

Since the temperature of the water should never rise above 142°, you will need to continually monitor the temperature during this process. Adjust the temperature settings on your stove as needed to accomplish this task.

Rinse the eggs with cold water. Carefully gather the eggs out of the water using a slotted spoon and rinse them under cold water until the shell drops down to room temperature or below.

Rinsing the eggs with cold water quickly drops the internal temperature of the egg, thereby preventing that temperature from continuing to rise or cook the egg.

Store the pasteurized eggs in your refrigerator. You can use them right away or continue storing them in your refrigerator for another week or so.

RECIPES

"Aged Eggnog" is becoming a thing of the modern era, and we have included one such recipe (imported from the Pacific Northwest) below as a reflection of the in situ evolution and contributions to this "aged tradition" from within our current culture.

ATLANTAN PROHIBITION-ERA MORNINGSIDE EGGNOG
The Hawk and the Owl
recorded by 1980

4 good eggs - *separated*

Beat yolks until thick with sugar and vanilla, to taste. Wash beaters, then beat whites until stiff. Whip cream. Fold whites into yolk and whipped cream.

Pour in some brandy or bourbon or somethin' extravagantly delicious! Serves 4-6

AMBASSADOR'S MORNING LIFT
Old Mr. Boston

1 qt. eggnog
6 oz. cognac
3 oz. Jamaican rum
3 oz. crème de cacao

Shake with ice until frothy and chilled; serve in a festive glass. Garnish with freshly-grated nutmeg.

A CLASSIC EGGNOG
Waldorf Astoria

1 egg
½ oz. simple syrup
2 oz. Royer Force 53 cognac -or-
    Pierre Ferrand 1840 cognac -or- 2 oz.

Brugal 1888 Gran Reserva rum -or- Ron Zacapa Gran Reserva -or- 2 oz. Baker's 107 proof bourbon -or- Henry McKenna 10 yr. old bourbon

1 oz. heavy cream *-or-* half-and-half
2 drops pure vanilla extract

Crack egg and place in a mixing glass. Add syrup and dry-shake until egg is broken and frothy. Add remaining ingredients and shake with ice until well incorporated and light. Double-strain into a chilled eggnog chalice. Garnish with freshly-grated nutmeg.

CHRISTMAS YULE EGGNOG
Old Mr. Boston

1 qt. eggnog
12 oz. strait whisky
1 ½ oz. rum

DRUMMER BOY
The Hawk and the Owl

inspired by DIY Bitters

1 Christmas mug of eggnog *as preferred basic recipe* -or- warm cider
1 tsp. Winter's Adventure bitters *{see below}*

Garnish with a stick of cinnamon

TO MAKE: "WINTER'S ADVENTURE" BITTERS

3 oz. birch bark tincture
1 ½ oz. orange peel tincture
1 oz. allspice tincture
1 oz. cinnamon tincture
1 oz. rosemary tincture
½ oz. clove tincture

Combine into an 8 oz. amber dropper bottle.

"FESTIVE GATHERING" EGGNOG
Jerry Thomas

(serves a party of forty imbibers)

1 dozen eggs
2 quarts brandy
1 pint Santa Cruz rum
2 gallons of milk
1 ½ lbs. white sugar

Separate the whites of the eggs from the yolks, beat them separately with an egg-beater until the yolks are thoroughly broken and frothy, and the whites assume a fleecy appearance. Mix all the ingredients (except the egg whites) in a large punch bowl, then let the whites float on top, and ornament with colored (green and red) sugars. Cool in a tub of ice, and serve. Garnish with freshly-grated nutmeg.

IMPERIAL EGGNOG
Old Mr. Boston

1 qt. eggnog
10 oz. brandy
2 oz. apricot brandy

Shake with ice until frothy and chilled; serve in a festive glass. Garnish with freshly-grated nutmeg.

KENTUCKY EGGNOG
Old Mr. Boston

1 qt. eggnog
6 oz. Kentucky bourbon
3 oz. brandy
3 oz. Jamaican rum

Shake with ice until frothy and chilled; serve in a festive glass. Garnish with freshly-grated nutmeg.

NASHVILLE EGGNOG

Old Mr. Boston

1 qt. eggnog
6 oz. Tennessee whiskey
3 oz. brandy
3 oz. Jamaican rum

Shake with ice until frothy and chilled; serve in a festive glass. Garnish with freshly-grated nutmeg.

AGED MESHUGGENOG

Originally entitled "AD's Infamous Egg Nog aka "Nog of the Gods" as given to Glenn Travis, passed down to his son Aaron, aka "Trav," and then bequeathed to Dan "The Man" Corcoran via Frank Young

HALF BATCH

(for full batch, double all ingredients)

6 eggs, separated
3⁄4 cups white sugar, *-or-* less
1⁄2 bottle rye whiskey *such as Old Overholt*
1⁄2 cup dark rum
1⁄2 cup brandy
3 cups milk, whole *-or-* 2%
1⁄2 cup heavy [whipping] cream

Beat egg yolks until pale yellow. Slowly add sugar to yolks until well dissolved. Separately, combine all the booze in a large bowl. SLOWLY add the egg/sugar mixture to the liquor bowl, allowing a jelly-like substance to form. Beat in milk. In [another] separate bowl, whip egg whites until they from soft peaks; [also in a separate bowl] whip cream until light and fluffy. Fold egg whites and whipped cream together by hand. Place in a large serving bowl. Slowly pour liquor mixture into egg whites/ cream. Cream will stay on top. Age for 3 months in the refrigerator. When ready to serve, grate fresh nutmeg over top. ENJOY.

SABBATH CALM

Waldorf-Astoria

1 egg
1⁄2 oz. simple syrup
3⁄4 oz. Cardenal Mendoza Solera Gran Reserva brandy *-or-* preferred brandy
3⁄4 oz. port wine
3⁄4 oz. French roast coffee, chilled
3⁄4 oz. heavy cream *-or-* half-and-half

Crack egg and place in a mixing glass. Add syrup and dry-shake until egg is broken and frothy. Add remaining ingredients and shake with ice until well incorporated and light. Double-strain into a chilled eggnog chalice. Garnish with freshly-grated nutmeg.

SHERRY EGGNOG

Jerry Thomas; Old Mr. Boston

1 tbsp. white sugar
1 egg
some milk
2 wine glasses of Rancho de Philo Triple Cream Sherry

Dissolve the sugar with a little water; break the yolk of the egg in a large glass; put in one-quarter tumblerful of broken ice; fill with milk, and shake up until the egg is thoroughly mixed with the other ingredients, then grate a little nutmeg on top; toast to the gods, and quaff the nectar cup.

SPICED EGGNOG
de la Foret

3 eggs
¼ cup raw local honey
2 tbsp. vanilla extract
1 tbsp. freshly-grated nutmeg
¼ tsp. cinnamon powder
¼ tsp. ginger powder
⅛ tsp. ground cloves
1 cup whipping cream
1 cup whole milk
½ cup dark rum *optional, but highly recommended!*

In a bowl whisk the eggs until they're very frothy (at least 2 minutes).

Whisk in the until until fully blended. Then add the vanilla, nutmeg, cinnamon, ginger, and cloves. Continue whisking.

Slowly and gently and in small amounts, whisk in the whipping cream, then the milk.

Finally, whisk in the rum. Store in a glass jar, chill for at least 1-2 hours before-serving. Stir before serving. Garnish with freshly-grated nutmeg.

WALDORF HOT EGGNOG
Waldorf-Astoria

5 oz. whole milk
1 tbsp. superfine sugar
1 egg yolk
2 oz. Bacardi anejo rum

Add milk to a saucepan and stir continuously over medium heat (do not boil). Add sugar to a ceramic mug. Dry-shake rum and egg for 5 seconds, then add to the cup topping with the hot milk. Stir to integrate. Garnish with freshly-grated nutmeg.

DRINKS

COFFEES

COCKTAILS

PUNCHES, BOWLS,
GROG, NEGUS,
MULLED WINES
AND CIDERS

POUSSES

SYLLABUBS

DRINKING CHOCOLATES,
ELIXIRS, AND TEAS

BACK BAR

COFFEES

FROM THE HAWK AND THE OWL, PRIVATE DRINKING HOUSE

SCRUMPTIOUSLY SPICED SINGLE-ORIGIN POUR-OVER COFFEE, NO. 1

Pour-over with an orange peel, a couple drops of vanilla extract, 3 broken pods of star anise, broken cinnamon stick

SCRUMPTIOUSLY SPICED SINGLE-ORIGIN POUR-OVER COFFEE, NO. 2

Pour-over with an orange peel, cinnamon, nutmeg, allspice, a couple drops vanilla extract, and pumpkin pie spices

SCRUMPTIOUSLY SPICED SINGLE-ORIGIN POUR-OVER COFFEE, NO. 3

After pouring-over, add ½ oz. of Italian Amaretto liqueur. Serve with 2 slices Elven bread (see pg. 101 for recipe).

SCRUMPTIOUSLY SPICED SINGLE-ORIGIN POUR-OVER COFFEE, NO. 4

Pour-over with wild cherry bark, birch bark, cinnamon bark, 1-2 whole clove. Serve with Lamb Sugarworks Dark Robust vanilla-bean-infused maple syrup, to taste.

SCRUMPTIOUSLY SPICED SINGLE-ORIGIN POUR-OVER COFFEE, NO. 5

After pouring over, add 1-2 oz. house-made eggnog, to taste. Serve with a simple less-sweet Christmas cookie, to preference.

SCRUMPTIOUSLY SPICED SINGLE-ORIGIN POUR-OVER COFFEE, NO. 8

(more suitably an evening coffee)

Before "coffee", slowly enjoy a glass of amotinallo sherry while building up the hearth fire. Then, after pouring-over coffee, add 1-2 oz. Tuaca to brew, to taste. Serve with a simple less-sweet Christmas cookie, to preference.

CAFÉ BRÛLOT

Joy, 1964; from New Orleans and of
French-Creole descent; Savoy

"This festive bowl requires a darkened room."

1 small orange
20 whole cloves
Peel of 1 orange, thinly sliced
Peel of 1 lemon, thinly sliced
2 sticks cinnamon, reverently broken
10 small cubes of sugar
¾ cup brandy -or- ¼ cup Cointreau
  + ¼ cup warm brandy -or- ¼ cup
  Cointreau
4 cups freshly-brewed coffee, par
  excellence

Wash the citrus well, then stud the orange
with the cloves. Place the orange and
lemon peels, cinnamon, and sugar in a
deep silver bowl. Heat (but do not boil)
the ¾ cup of brandy (or ¼ cup Cointreau),
and pour over the above. Place the bowl
on a tray or trivet and place the bowl,
orange, and a ladle on the serving table.
Ignite the brandy and ladle the mixture
repeatedly over the spices until the sugar
melts. Pour the coffee into the bowl.
Fill the ladle with the second portion of
brandy; tip the cloven orange carefully
into it, then ignite the liquor, and gently
lower the flaming ladle into the bowl,
floating the orange. Ladle the Café Brûlot
into demitasse cups. Garnish with a twist
of lemon.

IRISH COFFEE

Waldorf-Astoria

1 ½ oz. Irish whiskey
1 oz. Bailey's Irish cream -or- house-
  made Irish cream liqueur *at room
  temperature*
5 oz. fresh French roast coffee
Fresh whipped cream

Warm coffee glass with hot water. Let
stand for a minute then discard water.
Add ingredients in order listed, then stir
to integrate. Top with small amount of
house-made freshly-whipped cream.
Garnish with freshly-grated nutmeg
(optional). Serve with a spoon.

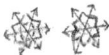

COCKTAILS

ADONIS, 1884
Waldorf-Astoria

1 ½ oz. Rancho de Philo
    Triple Cream Sherry
1 ½ oz. sweet vermouth
2 dashes Regans' Orange
    Bitters No. 6

Stir with ice and strain into chilled coupe.
Garnish with a twist of orange.

AFTER DINNER COCKTAIL
Savoy

½ prunelle brandy
½ cherry brandy
4 dashes fresh-squeezed lemon juice

Shake well with ice, then strain into a
sherry glass.

AMBROSIA ☆
Savoy

1 oz. Clavados
1 oz. best brandy
1 dash curaçao -or- orange liqueur
½ oz. fresh-squeezed lemon juice
champagne

Shake with ice, then strain over cubed ice
into a highball glass. Top with champagne!

AMPERSAND
Waldorf-Astoria

1 oz. Castarede Sélection Armagnac
    -or- Pierre Ferrand Ambre cognac
1 oz. Ransom Old Tom gin -or- Hay-
    man's Old Tom gin
1 oz. sweet vermouth
    oz. Pierre Ferrand dry curaçao -or-

Grand Marnier
2 dashes Bittermens Orange Cream
    Citrate -or- Regans' orange bitters
    No. 6

Stir with ice in mixing glass, then strain
into a chilled cocktail glass. Garnish with
a lemon peel.

ANGEL FACE
Savoy

⅓ dry gin
⅓ apricot brandy
⅓ Calvados

Stir well, then strain into a cocktail glass
over a few shards of hard ice.

APPLE + SPICE
18.21 Bitters

2 oz. good whiskey
½ oz. St. George Spiced Pear
½ 18.21 Apple Cardamom Shrub
½ oz. lemon juice
Topped off with 18.21 Ginger Beer

Mix and serve over ice.

APPLE-CARDAMOM MULE
Old 4th Distillery

2 oz. Old 4th Distillery Vodka
2 oz. unfiltered local apple cider
1 oz. 18.21 Bitters Cardamom Shrub
1 oz. 18.21 Bitters Ginger Beer Syrup
Splash of club soda

Shake with ice (excepting club soda), then
strain into an ice-filled mule mug. Top
with club soda. Garnish with a thin slice
of Georgia apple and a stick of cinnamon
-or- a slice of lime.

APPLE TODDY
Jerry Thomas

1 tbsp. fine white sugar
1 wine-glass of cider brandy
½ of a baked apple

Fill the glass two-thirds full of boiling water (insure glass is heat-proof!), and grate a little nutmeg on top.

APPLE MALT TODDY
Jim Meehan, PDT

2 oz. Red Jacket Orchards Apple Cider
1.5 oz. Chivas Regal 12-yr. old blended Scotch whisky
1 oz. Drouhin Pommeau
¼ oz. St. Elizabeth Allspice Dram
1 tsp. Lamb Sugarworks Dark Robust maple syrup

Heat everything and serve in a pre-warmed heat-proof mug. Garnish with cinnamon stick.

APRES-SKI MULLED WINE
French Alps, ski villages

Bottle of dry red wine
50 ml of brandy
1 orange
2 tbsp of honey or organic sugar
8 whole cloves
2 sticks of cinnamon
2 star anise

Squeeze orange into brandy, add sugar, cloves, cinnamon, and star anise seeds; let sit for a day or so. Then add to a superior dry red wine. Serve warm in a stemmed handle mulled-wine heat-proof glass.

COCKTAIL TERMINOLOGY

HOW DO YOU LIKE IT?

(A BRIEF OVERVIEW OF ORDER STYLES)

"NEAT"

served with no ice, straight out of the bottle

"UP"

chilled, and served in a cocktail glass

"ON THE ROCKS"

poured over one or more well-chosen cocktail-appropriate piece[s] of ice

WITH A "TWIST"

with a small strip of citrus peel

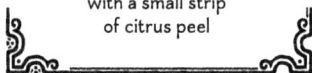

APRICOT FLIP
PDT

2 oz. cognac
¾ oz. Rothman & Winter Orchard Apricot
½ oz. simple syrup
1 egg

Dry-shake, then shake with ice and strain into a chilled fizz glass. Garnish with grated nutmeg.

THE ARCHBISHOP
Savoy adaptation of the Heruculean "Wow Cocktail"

¼ best rum
¼ high-quality sweet vermouth
¼ Calvados -or- Apple Brandy
¼ best brandy
Dash of Angostura bitters

Shake well with ice, then strain into a cocktail glass. Garnish with orange slice.

ARCTIC ARDSLEY
Waldorf-Astoria

1 oz. Plymouth gin
1 oz. Plymouth sloe gin
1 oz. Banal Quinquina Aperitif -or- cocchi Barolo Chinato
2 dashes Regans' orange bitters No.6

Stir in mixing glass with ice until chilled, then strain into a cocktail glass. Garnish with both the peels of orange and lemon.

AUTUMN SOLSTICE
(FOR THANKSGIVING!)
Waldorf-Astoria

2 o. Banks 7 Golden Age dark rum
¾ oz. Meletti amaro
¼ oz. fresh-squeezed lemon juice
3 dashes house-made Cinnamon Bitters -or- a hint of house-made Cinnamon Vodka

Stir with ice until chilled, then strain into a chilled cocktail glass. Garnish with orange peel. Serve with a scone and a generous scoop of house-made fig jam.

AVIATION
PRE-PROHIBITION
PDT, Waldorf-Astoria

2 oz. botanical gin
¾ oz. fresh-squeezed lemon juice
½ oz. Luxardo Maraschino Liqueur
¼ oz. crème de violette

Shake with ice and strain into a chilled coupe. Garnish with a brandied-cherry.

BAGPIPER
Waldorf-Astoria

1 ½ oz. Clove-infused Monkey Shoulder blended Scotch whisky
{see below}
1 oz. pomegranate liqueur
1 ½ oz. fresh-squeezed orange juice
3 cloves

Shake well with ice and strain into chilled cocktail glass. Garnish with a brandied cherry.

TO MAKE: CLOVE-INFUSED SCOTCH

Add 15 whole cloves to 750mL of Scotch whisky for two weeks. Fine-strain and funnel back into the bottle.

BAKED APPLE TODDY
Waldorf-Astoria

a 18th century wintertime classic

¼ warm baked apple *per serving*
1 Demerara sugar cube -or- tsp. Lamb Sugarworks maple syrup
2 oz. Laird's bonded applejack -or- Boulard Grand Solage VSOP calvados
6 oz. hot water

Rinse, peel, and core apple(s). Wrap in parchment paper (with a sprinkling of ground cinnamon, if preferred) and bake on a baking sheet at 350°F for 30-40 minutes. Add sugar cube to a ceramic mug and enough boiling water to dissolve. Snap lemon peel, and rub around rim of each cup then drop it in. Add baked apple portion and top with boiling water. Stir to break down the apple. Garnish with freshly-grated nutmeg.

BALTHAZAR
The Hawk and the Owl

Fernet Branca -or- **Royal Combier**
Best Pinot Noir, *chilled overnight prior*

To be imbibed on (and not excluding) January 6th, "whilst "chalking the door," & the 11th. Equal parts (to preference), served in an exquisite drinking vessel. Garnish with a thin slice of orange, then toast to the Babylonian Scholar.

"BALM OF GILEAD"
The Hawk and the Owl

2 oz. preferred gin
6 oz. fresh pomegranate juice
½ oz. **Pine Syrup** 🍸
4 oz. club soda
¼ oz. fresh-squeezed lime

Stir in a mixing glass, then pour into an ice-filled collins glass. Garnish with a sprig of fresh tender rosemary and a lime.

THE BAY RUM
Stewart

1 ½ oz. dark rum
½ oz. St. Elizabeth Allspice Dram -or- another pimento dram
½ oz. Velvet falernum
Dash of Angostura bitters
Fresh juice of a segment of tangerine -or-**orange**

Shake with ice, strain, then serve on the rocks in an Old-Fashioned glass.

BETSY ROSS
PDT

2 oz. cognac
¾ oz. Ruby port
½ oz. Grand Marnier
2 dashes Angostura bitters

Sir with ice and strain into a chilled coupe. Garnish with grated nutmeg.

BETTER TIMES
Hitchcock, 2010

1 oz. best rum
1 oz. Tuaca
½ oz. fresh-squeezed lime
½ oz. **House-made Grenadine** 🍸

Shake with ice, then strain into a chilled cocktail glass. Garnish with freshly-grated nutmeg.

BENTLEY
Savoy

½ Calvados
½ Dubonnet

Shake well with ice, then strain into a chilled cocktail glass.

BIJOU, 1895
Savoy, Waldorf-Astoria

1 ½ oz. botanical gin
1 oz. sweet vermouth
1 oz. green Chartreuse
1 dash orange bitters No.6

Stir with ice and strain into a chilled coupe. Garnish with a cherry and a lemon twist.

BIJOU, NO.2
PDT

1 ½ oz. Grand Marnier
1 oz. dry vermouth
1 dash Angostura bitters
1 dash orange bitters No.6

Stir with ice and strain into a chilled coupe.
Garnish with a cherry and a lemon twist.

BISHOP
PRE-PROHIBITION VERSION
Waldorf-Astoria

2 oz. white rum
1 oz. pinot noir
½ oz. fresh-squeezed lime juice
½ oz. house-made Demerara syrup
2 dashes pimento bitters -or- allspice
  dram

Shake with ice, then strain into a chilled
cocktail glass. Garnish with an orange
peel.

THE BITTER
SOUTHERNER NO.1
Jerry Slater

2 oz. Booker's Bourbon
½ oz. Fernet Branca
2 dashes Fee's Whisky Barrel-Aged
  Bitters
¾ oz. sorghum mix

Stir in a mixing glass with ice until chilled,
strain into a chilled coupe. Garnish with a
flamed orange peel.

THE BITTER
SOUTHERNER NO.3
Paul Calvert

3 dashes Peychaud's Bitters
½ oz. Gran Classico Bitter
¾ oz. Cynar

¾ oz. Carpano Antica Formula
  sweet vermouth
1 oz. Rittenhouse bottled-in-bond,
  100-proof rye whiskey
Dash of Herbsaint Legendre

First, fill a single rocks glass with ice and
pour in a very small quantity of Herbsaint
Legendre, then set it aside. Then, in a
chilled mixing glass the ingredients above.
Fill the mixing glass to the top with ice,
and stir for about 30 seconds. Roll the
rocks glass sideways to coat the inside of
the glass with the Herbsaint Legendre,
then pour out the contents. Strain the
drink from the mixing glass into the Herb-
saint-coated rocks glass.

Take a strip of lemon peel and squeeze it
to express its oils over the top of the drink,
then drop the peel into the drink.

THE BITTER
SOUTHERNER NO.4
Abigail Gullo

For celebration and exuberance.

2 oz. Rougaroux Full Moon Dark
  Rum, Old New Orleans Amber
  Rum, -or- Ron Zacapa Rum
½ oz. Averna
½ oz. Campari
1 tsp. Steen's Cane Syrup

Stir with cracked ice in a mixing glass until
chilled. Strain into a chilled cocktail glass.
Garnish with the twist of a grapefruit.

BLACKJACK
PDT, Waldorf-Astoria

1 ½ oz. cognac
½ oz. Clear Creek Kirschwasser
 -or- other cherry brandy
½ oz. excellent strongly-brewed
 coffee
¼ oz. Demerara syrup

Shake with ice and strain into chilled coupe.
Garnish with three cherries on a pick.

BLACKSTAR
PDT

2 oz. vodka
¾ oz. lime juice
¾ oz. grapefruit juice
¼ oz. Borsci Sambuca
¼ oz. simple syrup

Shake with ice and strain into a chilled
coupe. Garnish with a star anise pod.

BLACKSTRAP TIME TRAVELER TODDY
Waldorf-Astoria

⅓ oz. blackstrap molasses
2 oz. funky and assertive navy-
 strength rum
5 oz. hot water

Add molasses to ceramic mug and dissolve
with a bit of hot water. Add rum and top
with hot water, stirring again to integrate.
Garnish with freshly-grated nutmeg.

BLACKTHORN (ENGLISH)
PDT

1 ½ oz. botanical gin
¾ oz. sloe gin
¾ oz. sweet vermouth
2 dashes orange bitters

Stir with ice and strain into a chilled
coupe. Garnish with an orange twist.

"BLOOD AND SAND"
PDT, Savoy, Waldorf-Astoria

for the tinkering mixologist

1 ½ oz. blended Scotch whisky
¾ - 1 oz. fresh blood orange
½ - ¾ Cherry Heering *cherry brandy*
½ - ¾ oz. sweet vermouth

Shake with ice and strain into a chilled
coupe.

BLOOD ORANGE SIDECAR
Stewart

1 ½ oz. cognac -or- preferred brandy
¾ oz. fresh juice of a blood orange
½ oz. Orangerie -or- Soreno Blood
 Orange Liqueur
Dash of Angostura bitters

Shake (excepting bitters) with ice, then
strain into cocktail glass. Add dash of
bitters on top upon serving.

BLUE MOON
Old Mr. Boston

1 ½ oz. dry gin
¾ oz. Crème de Yvette
twist of lemon peel

Stir well with cracked ice and strain into 3
oz. cocktail glass. Garnish with a twist of
lemon peel.

BOILO
via Carrie Ferrence

*"a traditional Christmas or Yuletide drink in
the Coal Region of northeastern and east
central Pennsylvania. Boilo is a variation of a
traditional Lithuanian liqueur called 'Krupnik,'
or 'Krupnikas.'"*

ROBERT BURNS
PDT, Waldorf-Astoria

2 oz. Benromach 12-year old single malt Scotch whisky
¾ oz. Martini Sweet Vermouth
1 tsp. Bénédictine

Stir with ice and strain into a chilled coupe.

BOXING DAY SANTA
the Miracle Bar, Atlanta

23oz. mulled red wine
2 oz. tawny port
1 oz. orange liqueur
Dash of seasonal spices

Shake with ice, then strain into a wine-glass. Garnish with a stick of cinnamon.

BRADLEY-MARTIN,
Waldorf-Astoria
a Grasshopper without the cream

1 ½ oz. Tempus Fugit crème de menthe
1 oz. Tempus Fugit crème de cacao

Pour at equal times into an Old-Fashioned glass over crushed ice. Stir briefly to integrate.

BRANDY ALEXANDER
Savoy

1 oz. best brandy
½ oz. crème de cacao
1 oz. fresh cream

Shake well with ice until cream is light and frothy, then strain into a chilled champagne flute. Dust with nutmeg. Garnish with a twist of lemon.

BRANDY ALEXANDER, 1916
Waldorf-Astoria

1 ½ oz. Royer Force 53 -or- Pierre Ferrand 1840
1 oz. Marie Brizard White crème de cacao
1 oz. heavy cream -or- half-and-half
Slightest drop of real vanilla extract

Shake vigorously with ice and strain into chilled cocktail glass. Garnish with freshly-grated nutmeg -or- dark chocolate shavings.

BRANDY CRUSTA
PDT, Savoy, Schmidt, Old Mr. Boston, etc.

2 oz. cognac
¾ oz. freshly-squezed lemon juice
½ oz. Luxardo Maraschino Liqueur
½ oz. Marie Brizard orange curaçao
Dash of Angostura bitters

Shake with ice and strain into a chilled, lemon-and-sugar-rimmed wine glass filled with cracked ice and the peels of both a whole lemon and an orange.

BRANDY CRUSTA
Waldorf-Astoria

2 oz. Kelt VSOP Cognac
½ oz. Cointreau
¼ oz. house-made Demerara syrup
¼ oz. fresh-squeezed lemon juice
1 dash Angostura bitters
1 dash Peychaud's bitters

Rub a lemon rind along ½" rim of a wine-glass, small goblet, or brandy cocktail glass, then dab and roll in superfine sugar on a small plate. Peel an organic lemon in a long swath -or- an orange (whichever you prefer) an carefully curl round the inside of the glass in a becoming manner.

Add all ingredients to a mixing glass with ice and stir for 30 seconds until well-incorporated, then strain into the prepared glass.

BYCULLA
Savoy

2 oz. freshly-grated ginger juice shot
2 oz. curaçao
2 oz. best port
2 oz. best sherry

Shake well with ice, then strain into a tall wine-glass of Indian inspiration. Serve with almonds or macaroons.

"BY JOVE!"
PDT

2 oz. botanical gin
1 ½ oz. Carpano Antica Sweet
  Vermouth
¼ oz. Fernet Branca

Stir with ice and strain into a chilled coupe. Garnish with a twist of orange.

CAFE KIRSCH
Waldorf-Astoria

½ egg white
½ oz. simple syrup
1 oz. best brandy
1 oz. cherry brandy
1 oz. coffee

Add egg white and simple syrup to mixing glass. Dry-shake vigorously. Add remaining ingredients and shake with ice. Strain into chilled cocktail glass.

CARIBOU
Stewart

3 oz. red wine
1 ½ oz. whiskey -or- rye

1 oz. splash of port optional
1 oz. splash of sherry optional
1 oz. splash of brandy optional
1 tsp. Lamb Sugarworks Dark Robust
  maple syrup

Shake over ice until maple syrup is well incorporated, strain into old-fashioned glass.

THE CAROB ALGORITHM
Zachos

2 oz. pisco
½ oz. Carob Syrup 🍶
1 tsp. Spicebrush Dram 🍶
1 egg yolk
1 tsp. cream

Dry-shake until egg is light and fluffy, then shake with ice. Strain into a cocktail glass.

CHAMPAGNE COCKTAIL ☆
Waldorf-Astoria

1 sugar cube
2 dashes Angostura bitters
5 oz. brut champagne non-vintage
  -or- refined, dry Spanish cava

Place the cube of sugar on an elegant plate, splash with bitters. Place the anointed cube into a champagne flute, fill flute with champagne, twist a lemon peel to release oils, then discard.

CHAMPS-ELYSEES
PDT

2 oz. cognac
¾ oz. lemon juice
½ oz. green Chartreuse
¼ oz. simple syrup
1 dash Angostura bitters

Shake with ice and strain into a chilled coupe. Garnish with a twist of lemon.

CHARLEMAGNE
inspired by Waldorf-Astoria

1 oz. botanical gin *i.e. Bainbridge Distillery*
½ oz. Luxardo maraschino liqueur
1 dash Regan's Orange Bitters No. 6
a splash of 18.21 Blood Orange +
  18.21 Ginger Shrub

Serve in Collins glass, over ice. Garnish
with orange peel, lemon peel, and a
brandied-cherry.

CHARLOTTE TREUSE
Tasty n' Sons, 2011

1 oz. Plymouth Gin
1 oz. fresh-squeezed grapefruit
½ oz. green Chartreuse
1 oz. Imbue bittersweet vermouth

Shake with ice, then strain into a chilled
cocktail glass. Garnish with a slice of
grapefruit.

CHAUNCEY
Waldorf-Astoria

¾ oz. gin
¾ oz. Old rye whiskey -or- bourbon
  whiskey
¾ oz. cognac
¾ oz. Dolin de Chambery sweet
  vermouth -or Carpano Antica
2 dashes Regans' orange bitters No.6

Stir with ice, then strain into a chilled
cocktail glass. Garnish with a lemon peel
(if rye) -or- orange (if made with bourbon)

CHORUS LADY
Savoy

1 oz. dry gin
1 oz. Italian vermouth
1 oz. French vermouth
¼ of an orange, juiced

Stir well, then strain into a lovely glass.
Garnish with a slice of orange and a
cherry.

CHRISTMAPOLITAN
the Miracle Bar, Atlanta

1 ½ oz. vodka
1 oz. Elderflower liqueur
1 oz. dry vermouth
Spoonful of **house-made spiced
  cranberry sauce** 📖
Twig of freshly-picked tender
  Rosemary
¼ oz. fresh-squeezed lime juice

Mist preferred glass with Absinthe. Shake
with ice, then strain into glass. Garnish
with an additional twig of Rosemary 2"
above lip of glass.

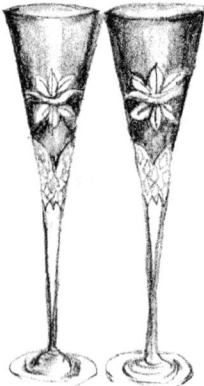

CHRISTMAS WALTZ
The Hawk and the Owl

3/4 oz. best bourbon
3/4 oz. best cognac
3/4 oz. best sweet vermouth
  -or- Carpano Antica
2 dashes of seasonal bitters -or-
  house-made aromatic bitters
1 egg white

Dry-shake until egg is light and frothy,
then shake with ice. Strain into an Old
Fashioned glass over one large cube of
ice, or to preference. Garnish with a slice
of lemon, 3 brandied cherries, and a
toasted marshmallow.

CHRIST'S ANTHEM
PDT

2 oz. Dolin Dry Vermouth
3/4 oz. Bénédictine
1/4 oz. Vieux Pontarlier Absinthe
1 dash orange bitters

Stir with ice and strain over a chilled
coupe. Garnish with a twist of orange

CINDERELLA'S CARRIAGE
Dietsh

2 oz. Laird's apple brandy
1/2 oz. Pumpkin Shrub 🧋
1/4 oz. allspice liqueur

Shake with ice, strain into chilled cocktail
glass. Garnish with freshly-grated nutmeg

COASTAL GEORGIAN
PDT

2 oz. rum
3/4 oz. lime juice
1/2 oz. crème de cacao
1/4 oz. sweet vermouth
1 tsp. House-made Grenadine 🧋

Shake with ice and strain into a chilled
coupe. Garnish with a lime wheel.

THE MYSTERIOUS "COFFEE COCKTAIL"
PDT, Waldorf-Astoria

as a perfect nightcap

1 1/2 oz. V.S.O.P Cognac
1 1/2 oz. Tawny port
1/4 oz. simple syrup
1 egg
*Dry-shake, then shake with ice and strain into
a chilled egg coupe. Garnish with freshly-grated nutmeg.*

COGNAC SOUR
18.21 Bitters

2 oz. best cognac
1/2 oz. 18.21 Tonic Syrup
1/2 oz. lemon juice
egg white
8-10 drops 18.21 Prohibition
  Aromatic Bitters

Mix and serve over ice.

COLE PORTER
Waldorf-Astoria

1 1/2 oz. straight rye whisky
1 oz. Rancho de Philo Triple Cream
  Sherry
3/4 oz. fresh lemon juice
1/2 oz. simple syrup
1 egg white

Dry-shake, then shake with ice and
strain into a chilled Collins glass filled
with Ice. Garnish with orange peel and a
brandied-cherry.

COMMODORE NO. 2
Waldorf-Astoria

1 ½ oz. Old 4th Bourbon
1 oz. Tempus Fugit crème de cacao
¾ oz. fresh-squeezed lemon juice
¼ oz. **House-made Grenadine**

Shake with ice, then strain into a chilled cocktail glass. Garnish with a lemon peel and a brandied-cherry.

THE CONQUISTADOR
Tasty n' Sons, 2011

2 oz. cold-press coffee
1 oz. Appleton white rum
¾ oz. Combier d'Orange
¾ oz. Tuaca
1 oz. cream, to whip
Dash of cinnamon

Shake the spirits and the coffee with ice; strain into a tall collins glass over rocks. Whip the cream, then pour over top. Serve with a long spoon and 2 Christmas cookies. Garnish with a sprinkling of freshly-ground cinnamon and a twist of orange.

CORONATION, NO.1
Waldorf-Astoria

1 oz. Laird's bonded applejack
 -or- VSOP cognac
1 oz. sweet vermouth
1 oz. extra dry vermouth
¼ oz. high-quality apricot liqueur

Shake with ice, then strain into an elegant cocktail glass. Garnish with an elegant peel of lemon.

CORONATION, NO.2
Savoy

⅔ best brandy
1 tbsp. *(a few dashes)* **curaçao**

1 dash peppermint bitters
1 dash peach bitters

Shake with ice, then strain into an elegant cocktail glass.

CRANBERRY COBBLER
PDT

2 oz. botanical gin
¾ oz. Lustau East India Sherry
½ oz. **Cranberry Syrup**
7 macerated cranberries *reserve three for garnish*
1 wheel of orange
1 wedge of lemon

Add the citrus, cranberries and syrup to a mixing glass and muddle. Add everything else, then shake with ice and strain into a chilled rocks glass filled with pebble ice.

Ganish with a sprig of mint and three macerated cranberries.

CREOLE CHRISTMAS
Savoy, David Wondrich

1 oz. rye whisky
1 oz. vermouth *to preference*
2 dashes Amer Picon -or- Amaro CioCiaro
2 dashes Bénédictine
dash of blood orange bitters
1 egg white

Dry-shake until egg is light and frothy, then shake with ice until chilled. Strain into a cocktail glass. Garnish with a lemon twist.

CREOLE LADY
Waldorf-Astoria

1 oz. Four Roses small-batch bourbon
1 oz. Sandeman Fine Rich Madeira
 -or- high-quality sipping sherry
½ oz. Luxardo maraschino liqueur

2 dashes Peychaud's bitters

Stir with ice, then strain into a chilled cocktail glass. Garnish with a brandied-cherry and a delightful lemon peel.

CRIMSON TIDE
PDT

1 1/2 oz. overproof rum
1 1/2 oz. **Spiced Sorrel** *(see below)*
3/4 oz. fresh-squeezed lime juice
1/2 oz. ginger liqueur

Shake with ice and strain into a chilled Collins glass filled with ice. Top with club soda. Garnish with a wheel of lime and a slender slice of candied ginger.

TO MAKE: SPICED SORREL

20 oz. water
about 7 pieces *(19.5 oz.)* of candied ginger
4 oz. superfine sugar
4 oz. dried sorrel flowers
2 cinnamon sticks
.2 oz. star anise pods
1/2 tsp. cloves

Combine everything in a pan and bring to a boil. Reduce to simmer and simmer for 20 minutes, stirring occasionally. Fine-strain, bottle, date, and store in the refrigerator

CUZCO
PDT

2 oz. Pisco
3/4 oz. Aperol
3/4 oz. simple syrup
1/2 oz. lemon juice
1/2 oz. juice of grapefruit

Shake with ice and strain into a chilled collins glass filled with ice (having first rinsed it with Clear Creek Kirschwasser). Garnish with a grapefruit twist.

DALMATIAN
Old 4th Distillery

2 oz. Old 4th Distillery Vodka
1/2 oz. Campari
2 oz. fresh ruby red grapefruit juice
1/2 oz. black pepper simple syrup
A few dashes Angostura bitters

Shake with ice, then strain into a chilled highball glass.

DE LA LOUISIANE
PDT

2 oz. rye whiskey
3/4 oz. sweet vermouth
3/4 oz. Bénédictine
3 dashes St. George Absinthe
3 dashes Peychaud's Bitters

Stir with ice and strain into a chilled coupe.Garnish with three brandied-cherries on a pick.

DEEP SOUTH'S SCUPPERNONG SOUR
Parsons

2 oz. Old 4th Bourbon
2 tbsp. scuppernong
  -or- muscadine jam
3/4 oz. fresh-squeezed lemon juice
1/4 oz. simple syrup
2 dashes 18.21 Bitters -or- Fee Brothers Whiskey Barrel-Aged Bitters
  -or-Angostura Bitters
1 egg white

Dry-shake until egg white is light and frothy, then shake with ice. Double-strain into a chilled old-fashioned glass or coupe.

DE RIGUEUR
Savoy

2 oz. best whisky, whichever kind is
  most currently preferred
1/2 oz. fresh grapefruit juice
1 tbsp. local honey

Shake well until honey is dissolved, then
strain over a large cube of ice into a
contemporary cocktail glass. Best with
fresh-squeezed juice.

EL DIABLO
PDT

2 oz. high-quality tequila
1 oz. ginger beer
3/4 oz. high-quality crème de Cassis
3/4 oz. fresh-squeezed lemon juice

Shake with ice and strain into a chilled
rocks glass filled with ice. Garnish with a
wheel of lemon and candied ginger.

DONIZETTI ☆
PDT

2 oz. botanical gin
1/4 oz. Amaro Ciociaro
1/4 oz. Rothman & Winter
  Orchard Apricot
champagne

Stir with ice and strain into a chilled
coupe. Top with champagne! Garnish
with a twist of lemon.

THE DOUGLAS
EXPEDITION
Stewart

1 oz. London dry gin
1 oz. Douglas fir eau-de-vie
1/2 St. Germain elderflower cordial
Juice of 1 wedge of lemon

Shake with ice, then serve in a cocktail

glass. Garnish with a thin slice of lemon.

DULCE DE LECHE
PDT

1 1/4 oz. high-quality tequila
3/4 oz. Toro Albala Pedro Ximenez
1/2 heavy cream
1 egg

Twist a grapefruit peel into a mixing tin.
Add everything else and dry-shake. Shake
with ice and strain into a chilled coupe.
Garnish with grated cinnamon.

THE DUKE
Waldorf-Astoria

2 1/2 oz. extra dry vermouth
1/4 oz. top shelf absinthe
1/4 oz. high-quality anisette
2 dashes Regan's Orange Bitters
  No. 6

Stir with ice, then strain into a chilled
cocktail glass. Garnish with a lemon peel.

DO YOU BELIEVE IN
MIRACLES?
Parsons

1 1/2 oz. vodka
3/4 oz. Clear Creek Douglas Fir eau
  de vie
1/4 oz. **Honey Syrup** 🗒
1/4 oz. **Rosemary Syrup** 🗒
2 dashes lavender bitters
2 drops -or- 4 spritzes of **Rosemary
  Tincture** {see below}

Combine all except tincture. Shake over
ice until chilled, then strain into a chilled
cocktail glass. Float Rosemary Tincture
atop. Garnish with rosemary sprig.

TO MAKE: ROSEMARY TINCTURE

½ cup fresh rosemary needles
1 cup high-proof vodka *80 to 100 proof*

Crush the needles using a mortar and pestle and transfer to a glass jar, cover with vodka, then put a lid on the jar and shake. Store in a cool, dark place. The alcohol will begin to turn green as it leaches oils from the rosemary. Shake and taste the infusion daily until it reached desired intensity (anywhere from a few days to 2 weeks). When the tincture is ready, strain through a funnel into a small eyedropper bottle or atomizer.

EL MOLINO
PDT

1 ½ oz. high-quality Mezcal
¾ oz. Rancho de Philo Triple Cream Sherry
¼ oz. St. Elizabeth Allspice Dram
¼ oz. high quality crème de cacao

Stir with ice and strain into a chilled coupe.

ENGLISH ROSE COCKTAIL
Old Mr. Boston

1 ¼ oz. dry gin *(i.e. Hendrick's)*
¾ oz. apricot brandy *(Marie Brizzard or similar, perhaps)*
¾ oz. dry vermouth
1 tsp. **House-made Grenadine** 📖
1 tsp. fresh-squeezed lemon juice
cherries

Frost rim of a 4 oz. cocktail glass by rubbing with lemon and dipping in sugar. Shake well with cracked ice and strain into frosted-rim glass. Serve with a cherry or two.

ESCARLATA
Starvation Alley Cranberry Juice Co.

recipe developed at Pelicano Restaurant, Ilwaco, WA

2 parts tequila
1 part Starvation Alley Cranberry Juice
1 part grapefruit simple syrup
1 part lime juice

Shake with ice, and pour over a large cube of ice.

ESPRESSO COCKTAIL
Waldorf-Astoria

2 ½ oz. **Coffee-Bean Vodka** 📖
¾ oz. simple syrup
¼ oz. high-quality anisette

Stir with ice, then strain into a chilled cocktail glass. Garnish with a lemon peel, if you so prefer.

THE EXPERIMENTAL
Alyce Tibbetts

2 oz. Booker's Bourbon
1 oz. Blanc Dolin Vermouth
1 oz. Cynar
1 oz. Rothman & Winter Orchard Apricot Liqueur
A few dashes of Fee Brothers Bitters

Build for two. Stir together, then pour equally between two Old Fashioned glasses, each over a one ice cube. Toast to a very enjoyable Friday evening and the inspiration the season brings.

FALL GIMLET
18.21 Bitters

2 oz. Old 4th Vodka
½ oz. 18.21 Rosemary Sage Syrup
½ oz. Suze Gentian Liqueur

½ oz. lime juice

Mix and serve over ice.

FASCINATION ☆
Waldorf-Astoria

2 oz. high-quality Absinthe
1 oz. Cointreau
champagne

Stir with ice, then strain into a champagne flute or a chilled cocktail glass with a large ice sphere. Top with champagne! Garnish with orange peel.

FA LA LA LA LA, LA LA LA LA
the Miracle Bar, Atlanta

1 oz. gin
½ oz. Aquavit
1 oz. hazelnut liqueur
¼ tsp. freshly-pounded cardamom, using mortar and pestle
¼ oz. vanilla extract
¼ oz. fresh-squeezed lemon juice
an egg white

Dry-shake egg white with all (excepting the gin and aquavit), then add other spirits and stir with ice. Strain into a chilled collins glass, top with club soda. Garnish with a few drops of house-made seasonal bitters.

FEZZIWIG'S RECLINE
Waldorf-Astoria

1 ½ oz. favorite bourbon
1 oz. favorite sweet vermouth
½ oz. favorite dry curaçao
¼ oz. **Cinnamon Vodka** 🍸
¼ oz. St. Elizabeth allspice dram
1 dash Angostura bitters

Stir with ice, then strain into a chilled cocktail glass. Garnish with orange peel.

LE FIN DE SIÈCLE, 1891
Schmidt

also called "William's Pride"

½ an orange, juiced
¼ a lemon, juiced
½ spoonful sugar
1 yolk of an egg *save egg white for the top*
½ oz. brandy
½ oz. Bénédictine
½ oz. maraschino liqueur
1 dash of curaçao
1 dash of anisette
1 dash of parfait amour
1 dash of noyeau
3 oz. pure cream

Shake well with ice until yolk is well-shaken and frothy. Strain into a fancy glass, then shake the egg white in a separate shaker with a little additional sugar until light and frothy. Gently ornament the cocktail with the egg white as if it were frozen snow, then decorate with a few drops of bitters, as preferred. Serve with a spoon.

FIN DE SIECLE
Waldorf-Astoria

a variation of the classic pre-dinner aperitif, the Bishop Poker

1 oz. Plymouth Gin

½ oz. sweet vermouth
½ oz. dry vermouth
¼ oz. Bigallet China-China Amer
   liqueur
2 dashes Regan's orange bitters

Stir with ice in a mixing glass. Strain into
a chilled cocktail glass. Garnish with the
peels of both a lemon and an orange.

FIRE CIDER HOT TODDY
Rosemary Gladstar via Han, de la Foret

¼ oz. raw local honey, to taste
¾ oz. **Fire Cider Immune Enhancer
   Tonic** *(see below)*
1 ½ oz. rye whiskey, mezcal -or- tequila reposado *whichever is preferred*

Shake together, then pour off into a
warmed mug. Top with hot water. Garnish
with a slice of lemon.

TO MAKE: FIRE CIDER IMMUNE
ENHANCER TONIC

½ cup *(about 10 cloves)* peeled, finely
   chopped garlic
½ cup *(about 4 oz.)* peeled, finely
   chopped horseradish
½ cup finely chopped [pungent
   yellow -or- brown] Vidalia -or- Walla
   Walla onion
¼ cup *(about 2 oz.)* peeled, finely
   chopped fresh ginger
¼ cup *(about 2 oz.)* peeled, finely
   chopped turmeric -or- 1 tbsp. fresh
   ground turmeric
1 small blood orange, quartered and
   thinly sliced crosswise
½ lemon, quartered and thinly sliced
   crosswise
1 habanero chile -or- 2 chiles pequis
   -or- ⅛ tsp. ground cayenne
½ tsp. black peppercorns
2-3 cups apple cider vinegar
2 tbsp. raw local honey, to taste.

Wash fruit thoroughly. Add everything but
vinegar into a sterilized 1L (quart) glass ball
jar. Pour vinegar across mixture, then stir
with a barspoon to allow vinegar to fill all
air pockets. Leave ½ headspace, insuring
that all ingredients are submerged.

Wipe the rim extraordinarily clean. Cover
jar with a non-reactive lid and store in a
cool dark place for one month, shaking
daily and checking that ingredients remain
submerged.

Fine-strain into a glass bowl, whisk in
honey. Transfer to sterilized bottle. May
store in refrigerator for up to 1 year.

FOX RIVER
Savoy

1 ½ oz. whisky -or- bourbon, of
   preference
½ oz. crème de cacao
4 dashes peach bitters
1 tsp. fresh-squeezed lemon juice

Shake with ice, then strain into a wine-
glass. Garnish with a lemon peel.

THE FRANCIS
Steven Savage, Tipsy Parson

1 oz. Fernet Branca
1 oz. Aged moscato grappa
1 oz. Carpano Antica (Red vermouth)
½ tsp. Bénédictine
2 dashes Peychaud's Bitters

Stir with ice and strain into a rocks glass
or over an ice cube. Garnish with a lemon
twist.

FRENCH "75" ☆
Craddock, PDT, Waldorf-Astoria

2/3 - 1oz. delightfully enchanting
   botanical gin
1/3 -1/2 oz. fresh-squeezed lemon juice
1 spoonful powdered sugar -or- 1/2 oz.
   simple syrup
champagne

Shake with ice, then strain into a chilled
champagne flute. Top with champagne!
Twist lemon to release oils, then discard.

GARLAND
Dietsh

2 oz. botanical -or- classic London
   dry gin
1 oz. **Cranberry Sauce Shrub** 🖾
1/2 oz. Plymouth sloe gin

Shake with ice, then strain into a chilled
cocktail glass or serve over one large ice
cube.

GILCHRIST
PDT

1 1/4 oz. blended Scotch whisky
3/4 oz. Clear Creek Pear Brandy
3/4 oz. grapefruit juice
1/2 oz. Averna Amaro
2 dashes grapefruit bitters

Shake with ice and strain into a chilled
coupe. Garnish with a twist of lemon.

GIN GENIE
Dietsh

2 oz. London dry gin
3/4 oz. **Fresh Ginger Shrub** 🖾
3/4 oz. **Lemon-Lime Shrub** 🖾
1/2 oz. Grand Marnier -or- Chartreuse

Shake with ice, then strain into chilled
cocktail glass, serve over ice. Garnish with

crystalized ginger and a brandied-cherry
on a pick.

GIN AND PINE
Jerry Thomas, classic

Split a piece of the heart of a green pine
log into fine splints, about the size of a
cedar pencil, take 2 ounces of the same
and put into a quart decanter, and fill
the decanter with gin. Let the pine soak
for two hours, and the gin will be ready
to serve.

GINGER COLLINS
FEBRUARY MEDICINAL
Waldorf-Astoria

2 oz. **Ginger and Lemongrass-
   infused Gin** 🖾
3/4 oz. fresh-squeezed lemon juice
1/2 oz. simple syrup
1 egg white

Dry-shake together until ingredients are
well-mixed. Add ice and shake further
until egg whites feel ready. Strain into
ice-filled Collins glass. Top with club soda.
Garnish with a brandied-cherry.

GINGER TODDY
The Hawk and the Owl

2-3 oz. Makers' Mark -or- bourbon
   of choice
1 tbsp. local honey
1/4 fresh-squeezed lemon juice
1/4" freshly-grated ginger
Pinch of cayenne *optional*

Top with piping hot water, stir, serve with
a spoon. Toast "to your good health"
and enjoy!

GINGERBREAD-MAN COCKTAIL
Waldorf-Astoria

1 ½ oz. **Vanilla Bean-infused Original Dark Rum** 🍷
¾ oz. **Cinnamon Vodka** 🍷
¾ oz. heavy cream -or- half-and-half,
½ oz. Monin gingerbread syrup*
{taste and adapt}

Shake thoroughly with ice, then strain into a chilled cocktail glass. Garnish with freshly-grated nutmeg.

GIRL FROM JEREZ
PDT

1 oz. Rhum Clement V.S.O.P.
1 oz. Mae de Ouro Cachaca
¾ oz. lime juice
½ oz. Lustau Pedro Ximenez
1 tsp. St. Elizabeth Allspice Dram

Shake with ice and strain into chilled coupe. Garnish with grated nutmeg.

GOLDEN SPIKE
via Demi Rasmussen

6 oz. fresh-squeezed orange juice
2 oz. Preferred vodka of choice

Shake with ice, then strain into a collins glass, top with club soda. Garnish with a wedge of orange.

GRASSHOPPER
Old Mr. Boston

¾ oz. green crème de menthe
¾ oz. white crème de cacao
¾ oz. light sweet cream

Pour ingredients into a cocktail shaker with cracked ice. Shake briskly, then strain into a chilled 3 oz. cocktail glass.

To make an "After Eight," add a layer of dark chocolate liqueur to the crème de menthe, crème de cacao, and cream.

To await the visitation of St. Nick (for adults only), substitute peppermint schnapps for the crème de menthe.

GREAT SECRET
Savoy

1 ½ oz. dry gin
¾ oz. "Kina Lillet"
dash of Angostura bitters

Chill gin. Stir all together, then pour into a cocktail glass. Garnish with orange peel.

GREEN DEACON
PDT

1 ½ oz. Plymouth Gin
1 oz. grapefruit juice
¾ oz. Plymouth sloe gin

Shake with ice and strained into an a St. George Absinthe-rinsed coupe.

HONEYMOON COCKTAIL
PDT, Savoy

2 oz. Laird's Bonded Apple Brandy
½ oz. orange curaçao
½ oz. Bénédictine
½ oz. fresh-squeezed lemon juice

Shake with ice, strain into a chilled coupe.

HOO HOO'S "OL' TANNEBAUM," ATLANTA 1892
The Hawk and the Owl

{the recipe for this concatenated cocktail of great forestry fellowship has been, to our knowledge, shrouded in mystery since circa 1826, but will be released by December 15th, 2026 in Piedmont Park, in honor to the members of its fraternal Order}

HOT WHISKEY SLING
Jerry Thomas

1 wineglass of whiskey

Fill tumber one-third full with boiling water, and grate nutmeg on top.

HOW THE GIMLET STOLE CHRISTMAS
the Miracle Bar, Atlanta

1 ½ oz. gin
1 oz. Pine-Caraway-Sage Cordial

Stir with ice, then strain into a chilled cocktail glass.

THE HUNGARIAN ☆
PDT

1 ½ oz. Clear Creek Plum Brandy
¾ oz. fresh-squeezed lime juice
½ oz. Zwack
½ oz. honey syrup
champagne

Shake with ice and strain into chilled egg coupe. Top with champagne! Garnish with a spritz of Marivani lavender essence and an edible orchid.

IMPROVED CAPE CODDER
Starvation Alley Cranberry Juice Co.

recipe developed at Raven + Rose, Portland, OR by David Shenaut

3 parts vodka
2 ½ parts Starvation Alley Cranberry Juice
1 part cane syrup
1 tsp. Campari

Build on ice, stir, squeeze lime. Garnish and sprinkle with coarse sea salt.

IMPROVED WHISKEY COCKTAIL
PDT

2 oz. rye whiskey
¼ oz. Luxardo Maraschino Liqueur
¼ oz. simple syrup
2 dashes Angostura bitters

Stir with ice and strain over one large cube into a chilled rocks glass (having been rinsed with Vieux Pontarlier Absinthe). Garnish with a twist of lemon.

JABBERWOCK
Savoy

⅓ dry gin
⅓ dry sherry
⅓ Caperitif
2 dashes orange bitters
a hint of fresh-squeezed lemon

Stir with ice, then strain into a cocktail glass. Garnish with a lemon peel.

JACK ROSE
Stewart, Savoy

1 ½ oz. applejack -or- Calvados
½ fresh-squeezed lemon juice
½ oz. House-made Grenadine 🍯

Shake with ice, then strain into a cocktail glass.

JACQUEMOT
PDT, Waldorf-Astoria

2 oz. Laird's Bonded Apple Brandy
¾ oz. lemon juice
¾ oz. **House-made Grenadine** 📖

Shake with ice and strain into a chilled coupe.

JADED GRASSHOPPER
Waldorf-Astoria

1 oz. **house-made Vanilla Vodka** 📖
1 oz. Drambuie liqueur
½ oz. Tempus Fugit crème de cacao
½ oz. green crème de menthe
1 oz. heavy cream -or- half-and-half, as preferred

Shake thoroughly with ice until cream is smooth, light, and frothy (may add a few sprigs of mint during preparation to add complexity, if inspired). Strain into a chilled cocktail glass. Double-straining will allow a luxuriously smooth trip across the palate. Garnish with chocolate shavings.

JIMMIE ROOSEVELT ☆
PDT

1 oz. V.S.O.P. Cognac
1 Demerara sugar cube soaked in Angostura bitters
1 tsp. green Chartreuse
champagne

Stir the Cognac with ice and strain into a chilled egg coupe filled with three cracked ice cubes. Add a sugar cube soaked with Angostura Bitters and top with champagne. Float the Green Chartreuse on the surface of the drink.

JINGLE BALL NOG
the Miracle Bar, Atlanta

½ oz. cognac
½ oz. amontillado sherry
1 tsp. peanut butter
Splash almond milk
½ cup Pandan-infused Cream, whipped
Nougat Syrup 📖
1 Egg

Dry-shake until egg is light and frothy, then add the peanut butter, then shake with ice until chilled. Strain into a tall cocktail glass. Garnish with freshly-grated nutmeg.

JOLLY OLD ENGLAND
The Hawk and the Owl

4-6 oz. fresh pomegranate juice
3-5 oz. house-made -or- Fever Tree Ginger Ale -or- soda water

Served in a tall collins glass over plentiful ice with a splash of delicious botanical gin. Garnish with a wedge of lime.

KAPPELER'S, 1895
PDT

2 oz. Laird Bonded Apple Brandy
¼ oz. green Chartreuse
¼ oz. Bénédictine
2 dashes Angostura bitters

Stir with ice and strain into chilled coupe.

KINA MIELE
PDT

1 oz. Dolin Dry Vermouth
¾ oz. Cocchi Americano
½ oz. Nonino Gioiello
¼ oz. Clear Creek Pear Brandy
1 dash Lemon Bitters

Stir with ice and strain over one large cube into a chilled rocks glass. Garnish with a grapefruit twist.

KING BEE
PDT

1 1/2 oz. Pisco
3/4 oz. lemon juice
1/2 oz. Bénédictine
1/2 oz. Barenjager

Shake with ice and strain into a chilled coupe. Float 1/2 oz. Rancho de Philo Triple Cream Sherry on the surface of the drink.

KIR ROYALE ☆
Stewart, classic

1 oz. crème de cassis
4 oz. champagne!

Pour the cassis into a champagne flute, then top with champagne!

KIR ROYALE, ADAPTED ☆
Dietsh

champagne
1/2 oz. shrub of choice *the classic Kir of Paris uses crème de cassis aka black currant liqueur*

Add shrub to champagne flute. Top with champagne!

KNUSPERHAUS
The Hawk and the Owl

1 oz. Gingerbread-Infused Bourbon
1 oz. Asbach Uralt cognac
1/2 oz. Killepitsch liqueur
1/4 oz. Rumple Minze
1 egg white

Dry-shake until egg is light and frothy, then shake with ice. Double-strain into a fun-and-festive glass over a large cube of ice. Garnish with a sprinkling of superb fair-trade cocoa powder -and- cinnamon powder

Serve with several German Bahlsen Lebkuchen Christmas cookies on a cut-glass plate.

KRAMPUS FLIP
The Hawk and the Owl

3/4 oz. chilled Green Chartreuse
1 oz. Rancho de Philo Triple Cream Sherry -or- best port
1/4 oz. House-made Grenadine 🍷
1 organic egg white

Pour the Green Chartreuse into a stemmed glass. Shake together with cracked ice the remaining ingredients, strain and float on top. Garnish with 2 spiked brandied-cherries.

THE LAST DROP
Waldorf-Astoria

2 oz. barrel-aged gin
3/4 oz. fresh-squeezed lemon juice
1/2 oz. simple syrup
1/4 oz. Clear Creek Cassis *blackcurrant liqueur*

Shake (all except cassis) with ice, then strain into a chilled cocktail glass. Drip cassis into center of the drink, causing it to pool at the bottom.

LAST WORD
PDT

3/4 oz. botanical gin
3/4 oz. Luxardo Maraschino Liqueur
3/4 oz. green Chartreuse
3/4 oz. lime juice

Shake with ice, strain into a chilled coupe.

L'ESPRIT DE NOËL, ELIXIR DE VIE NO.3
The Hawk and the Owl

Variation of the 1800s' classic St. Peter's Gimlet

1 oz. Clear Creek Douglas Fir Eau
de Vie -or house made Douglas Fir
Liqueur
2 oz. Greenhook Ginsmiths
American dry gin
3/4 oz. simple syrup
3/4 oz. fresh-squeezed lime juice
*Shake well with ice, then strain into chilled
cocktail glass. Garnish with a thinly sliced
lime wheel.*

L'ESPRIT DE NOËL, ELIXIR DE VIE NO.4
The Hawk and the Owl

Variation of a classic Manhattan

1 oz. Clear Creek Douglas Fir Eau
de Vie -or house made Douglas Fir
Liqueur
2 oz. rye whiskey, of preference
1 oz. vermouth *sweet -or- dry, to preference, try the sweet first*
1/2 oz. cherry liqueur *optional*
2 dashes bitters, of preference
*angostura -or- orange -or- other
try angostura for winter nights*

Shake well with ice, then strain into chilled
cocktail glass. Garnish with a brandied
cherry, or lemon peel.

LINDEN HEIGHTS
Alyce Tibbetts

2 oz. Basil Hayden's Bourbon Whisky
1 oz. Apertivo Cocchi Americano
1 oz. Rancho de Philo Triple Cream
Sherry

Stir together, then strain into an Old
Fashioned glass over 3 cubes of ice.

LOCOMOTIVE
Jerry Thomas, Waldorf-Astoria

12 cloves

2 cinnamon sticks
1 750mL bottle good red wine
4 egg yolks
4 house-made honey syrup
4 oz. Grand Marnier -or- curaçao

Warm (simmer, but do not boil) the
Burgundy in a pyrex double-boiler/
saucepan. Whisk (or shake) the egg yolks
add with the honey syrup and spices. Fine-
strain into a pitcher along with the good
red wine warmed to perfection. Serve hot
in warmed heatproof glasses or ceramic
cups. Garnish with freshly-grated nutmeg.

> "The only thing better than
> singing is more singing."
>
> —ELLA FITZGERALD

LONDON'S LITTLE APPLET PROTEGE
PDT

1 1/2 oz. 7-yr old Rum
1 oz. J.K. Scrumpy's Apple Cider
3/4 oz. fresh-squeezed lemon juice
1/2 oz. Demerara syrup

Shake with ice and strain into a chilled
Collins glass filled with pebble ice.
Garnish with a lemon-basted slice of
apple, sprinkle with grated cinnamon and
nutmeg.

THE LONG HELLO ☆
Parsons

3/4 oz. Clear Creek Apple Brandy
3/4 oz. St. Germain
Elderflower Liqueur
1 dash barrel-aged bitters -or- old
fashioned aromatic bitters
champagne

Stir with ice and strain into chilled coupe. Top with champagne! Garnish with grated nutmeg.

LORD BALTIMORE HOTEL
PDT

2 oz. rye whiskey
½ oz. Apple Brandy
½ oz. green Chartreuse

Stir with ice and strain into a chilled coupe.

MAE WEST ROYAL DIAMOND FIZZ, 1934 ☆
PDT, Waldorf-Astoria

(variation on the original)

2 oz. **Goji Berry-infused Four Roses Single Barrel Bourbon** *(see below)*
1 oz. grapefruit juice
½ oz. Pama Pomegranate Liqueur
1 egg
champagne

Dry-shake, then shake with ice and strain into a chilled egg coupe rimmed with sugar, cayenne, and cocoa powder. Top with champagne. Garnish with three whiskey-soaked goji berries on a pick.

TO MAKE: GOJI BERRY-INFUSED FOUR ROSES SINGLE BARREL BOURBON

1.6 oz. Goji Berries
1 750mL bottle Four Roses Single Barrel Bourbon

Combine the Goji Berries and whiskey in a non-reactive container. Infuse, covered, for 48 hours at room temperature. Fine strain and bottle.

MAJ JONG
Savoy

⅙ Cointreau
⅙ best rum
⅔ best dry gin

Stir well, then strain into a delightful cocktail glass before settling into ye olde winter games.

MANHATTAN, A SOUTHERNER'S TAKE
(built inversely)

2 dashes bitters
1 over-full oz. sweet vermouth
1 ½ oz. regionally-local -or- southern whisk[e]y *bourbon, blended, rye, -or- Canadian*

Built directly into a Manhattan glass over quite a few good rocks. Stir well to incorporate. Garnish with a cherry.

MAPLE CRANBERRY BOURBON MARTINI
Starvation Alley Cranberry Juice Co.

2 parts Starvation Alley Cranberry Juice
1 part bourbon
½ part maple syrup

Shake with ice, strain and serve up!

MARCHÉ DE NOËL
The Hawk and the Owl

1 oz. E. Giffard crème de Mirabelle
  cherry plum
4 oz. Pinot Gris -or- Cremant d'Alsace

Shake well with ice, then strain into a lovely wine glass. Garnish with a sugared plum. Serve with 2 bredele (spicy Christmas cookies) and a slice of house-made quiche lorraine.

MCELHONE'S OLD-SCHOOL ORIGINAL, 1929
PDT

2 oz. gin
3/4 oz. Cointreau
3/4 oz. fresh-squeezed lemon juice
1/4 oz. simple syrup
1 egg white

Dry-shake, then shake with ice and strain into a chilled egg coupe.

THE MEDICINAL
The Hawk and the Owl

Good part local honey
Better part favored whiskey
A kind amount of fresh-squeezed lemon
A touch of piping hot water, to balance.

Serve in a ceramic mug or heat-proof handled glass with a spoon for imbiber to stir frequently.

THE MERRY BERRY
Starvation Alley Cranberry Juice Co.

3 parts gin
1 1/2 parts Starvation Alley Cranberry Juice
1 part fresh lemon juice
1 part fresh orange juice
1 part rosemary simple syrup

Combine all ingredients, add ice, and top with soda water. Garnish with a sprig of rosemary and enjoy!

THE MERRY CHAT
Schmidt, classic

Bring to a boil a large pot of mixed tea; add a little sugar in the bottom of 2 pre-heated cups; fill each 2/3 with tea and top with best Burgundy; stir with an emptied vanilla bean pod (saved from another recipe at another time). Serve piping hot with some nibbles and good conversation.

THE MERRY GARDENER
Waldorf-Astoria, classic

over-wintered variation

1 1/2 oz. Byrrh Grand quinquina aperitif *Maurin quina -or- Dubonnet*
1 1/2 oz. Dolin dry vermouth
1/4 oz. Luxardo maraschino liqueur
   -or- Grand Marnier
1 dash orange bitters

Stir with ice, then strain into chilled cocktail glass. Garnish with two bran-died-cherries.

THE MERRY WOLVERINE ☆
The Hawk and the Owl

1 part **House-made Grenadine** 🏷
1 part **bourbon**
splash of simple syrup
freshly-grated ginger, to taste
dash of bitters
a hint of freshly-squeezed orange
   juice -or- lemon -or- both
1/3 part dry champagne

Add ingredients in order to wine glasses, drop in 2 non-sugary cherries, a sprig of green, and top with champagne!

Makes an excellent apres-ski celebratory drink for a merry group.

THE MERRY WOODSMAN
Zachos

3 oz. **Spruce Tip Vodka** 🍶
1 ½ oz. **Spruce Tip Syrup** 🍶
¾ oz. **St. Germain**
   Elderflower Liqueur
1 ½ tsp. **Ginger Syrup** 🍶

Shake with ice, then strain into a highball glass. Top with seltzer. Garnish with a sprig of spruce, if desired.

MIDNIGHT EXPRESS
PDT

3 oz. freshly brewed coffee
1 ½ oz. **Walnut-infused V.S.O.P.**
   Cognac 🍶
¼ oz. Luxardo Amaretto
¼ oz. simple syrup

Build in a preheated heat-proof mug. Garnish with freshly whipped cream and grated nutmeg.

MIDWINTER'S MOON
PDT

1 ½ oz. rye whiskey
1 oz. Lillet Blanc
½ oz. Laird's Bonded Apple Brandy
¼ oz. green Chartreuse
3 dashes Abbott's Bitters

Stir with ice and strain into a chilled coupe. Garnish with a twist of orange.

MIDWINTER'S SLING
PDT

1 ½ oz. Laird's Bonded Apple Brandy
½ oz. sweet vermouth
½ oz. Bénédictine
½ oz. Cherry Heering
½ oz. lemon juice
½ oz. ginger beer

Shake with ice and strain into a chilled

Collins glass. Garnish with a cherry and and a wedge of orange.

THE MODERN, NO. 62
inspired by Waldorf-Astoria

2 oz. Bainbridge Distillery botanical gin
1 oz. Sacred Spiced English Vermouth -or- Dolin Dry

Stir with ice, then strain (over a cinnamon stick) into a chilled Martini glass. Garnish with a lemon peel and a sightly sprig of juniper. Serve with lightly-toasted shaved almonds -or- big, bold, perfectly-balanced green olives.

MODERN TAKE ON THE AMARETTO SOUR
Jeffrey Morgenthaler

1 ½ oz. fine Italian amaretto liqueur
¾ oz. best cask-proof bourbon
1 tsp. simple syrup
1 oz. fresh-squeezed lemon juice
1 egg white

Dry-shake until egg is light and frothy, then shake with ice until chilled. Strain over fresh ice into an Old Fashioned glass. Garnish with 2 brandied cherries and a flamed-twist of lemon

MONT BLANC FIZZ
Waldorf-Astoria

2 oz. chilled club soda
2 oz. St. George Absinthe Verte
1 oz. orgeat syrup
1 egg white

Add chilled club soda to a small Collins glass or Fizz glass. Add remaining ingredients to a mixing glass. Dry-shake until incorporated, then shake with ice. Strain into glass over club soda. Stir quickly with bar spoon, then serve up.

MOUNT VERNON
PDT

1 oz. Clear Creek Kirschwasser
1 oz. Gran Duque D'Alba Brandy de Jerez
¾ oz. fresh-squeezed grapefruit juice
½ oz. Lustau Pedro Ximenez Sherry
½ oz. Cherry Heering

Shake with ice and strain into a chilled coupe. Garnish with three brandied cherries on a pick.

MRS. WHEELBARROW'S WINTER MARTINEZ
Dietsh

2 oz. London dry gin
1 oz. Carpano Antica -or- Punt e Mes sweet vermouth
½ oz. **Fig-Cinnamon Shrub** {see below}
1 thin orange peel

Shake with ice, then strain into a chilled cocktail glass. Twist the orange peel over an open flame to singe the oils. Drop into the glass.

TO MAKE: FIG-CINNAMON SHRUB

1 pint purple figs, pureed in a blender
1 cup apple cider vinegar
1-2 cinnamon sticks *to preference*
1 cup turbinado sugar

Combine all ingredients (excepting the sugar and starting with less cinnamon) in a non-reactive container and allow to sit at room temperature for 2 days. Stir and taste (add more cinnamon, if preferred, and allow to steep another day, if so). Strain and pour into a clean jar with the sugar and shake until well-dissolved. Allow to sit for at least a week before using. Store in the refrigerator for 1-2 weeks (or so, depending).

MULETIDE
the Miracle Bar, Atlanta

1 oz. Mezcal
1 oz. amontillado sherry
Allspice Dram, to preference
¼ tsp. freshly-grated ginger
¼ oz. fresh-squeezed lemon juice

Shake with ice, then strain into a cocktail glass. Garnish with 2 brandied cherries.

MULLED BRAMBLE
The Permit Room, London 2017

2 oz. mulled wine reduction
1 oz. Old Tom gin
½ oz. simple syrup
½ oz. fresh-squeezed lemon

Stir in a mixing glass until incorporated, then strain into a chilled martini glass. Dust with festive sugar-spices.

NTH DEGREE
PDT

1 oz. V.S.O.P.
1 oz. Laird's Bonded Apple Brandy
½ oz. green Chartreuse
1 Demerara sugar cube
2 dashes whiskey barrel aged bitters

Muddle the sugar cube and the bitters. Add everything else, then stir with ice and strain over one large ice cube into a chilled rocks glass. Garnish with an orange and a twist of lemon.

NATALE DOLCE
Waldorf-Astoria

1 oz. Spiced Rum -or- preferred brandy
1 oz. Varnelli Punch all Fiamma
   liqueur
1 ½ oz. Moccia Zabov zabaglione
   liqueur

Shake with ice, double-strain into
Old-Fashioned glass filled with large
ice cubes or sphere. Garnish with
freshly-grated nutmeg. Serve with French
vanilla tuile wafer -or- cocoa batons.

NEW YEAR'S DAY
APEROL SPRITZ
Todd Atlas

an aperitif to New Year's Day brunch

3 oz. Aperol
2 oz. most enjoyable Prosecco
1 oz. club soda
½ oz. fresh-squeezed orange juice

Stir Aperol and juice together, pour into
chilled rocks or wine glass, then fill with
ice; top with Prosecco, and then a splash
of club soda. Garnish with a thinly-sliced
half-wheel of orange.

NIGHTCAP
Waldorf-Astoria

2 oz. aged rum
1 oz. Grand Marnier
1 egg yolk
⅓ oz. heavy cream *optional*

Shake well with ice until egg yolk is light
and airy. Strain into a chilled cocktail glass.

NIGHT CAP
Savoy

1 oz. best brandy
1 oz. anise liqueur

1 oz. curaçao
1 egg yolk

Shake well with ice until yolk is light and
airy. Strain into a chilled cocktail glass.

NOCE ROYALE ☆
PDT

1 ½ oz. botanical gin
½ oz. sloe gin
¼ oz. Monteverdi Nocino
champagne

Stir with ice and strain into a chilled
coupe. Top with champagne!

NORTHERN LIGHTS
Waldorf-Astoria

1 ¼ oz. cognac
¾ oz. Aalborg akvavit
½ oz. Tempus Fugit crème de cacao
½ oz. Cocchi Americano Bianco

Stir with ice, then strain into chilled
cocktail glass. Garnish with a lemon peel.

NORWEGIAN
OCCIDENTAL
PDT

2 oz. Linie Aquavit
¾ oz. Grand Mariner
½ oz. Nonino Amaro

Stir with ice and strain into a chilled,
Fernet-Branca-rinsed coupe. Garnish with
a twist of orange and a brandied cherry
with long stem intact.

NUMBER THREE
Waldorf-Astoria

2 oz. botanical gin
¾ oz. Dolin Dry Vermouth
¼ oz. anisette
1 dash orange bitters

Stir with ice, then strain into chilled
cocktail glass. Garnish with a lemon peel.

THE NUTTY ITALIAN
Marjorie's

2 oz. Bulleit Bourbon
1 oz. Sidetrack Distillery Nocino
Dash of orange bitters

Shake with ice, then strain into a
Manhattan glass. Garnish with a thinly-
sliced peel of orange.

OLD FASHIONED
(MID-TWENTIETH-CENTURY
VERSION), ORIG. 1806 LOUIS-
VILLE, KENTUCKY

Todd Atlas

1 thin orange slice *half-wheel*
1 thin orange peel *for garnish*
2 brandied cherries
1 Demerara sugar cube -or- 2 tsp.
  2:1 Demerara simple syrup (to
  preference)
2 dashes Angostura bitters
1 dash orange bitters
2 ½ oz. Elijah Craig 12-yr. Old single
  barrel Bourbon -or- other preferred
  Bourbon

Squeeze the juice from the half-wheel
orange slice into an Old-Fashioned glass.
Toss it into the glass, and with a few quick
gentle taps with a muddler release the
juices without macerating to a mush.
Remove the orange peel and discard. Add
sugar cube. Shake the bitters onto the
sugar cube to help dissolve (alternatively
use a Demerara simple syrup). Add
whiskey and stir, making sure the sugar is
dissolved and evenly distributed. Add a
few large ice cubes and stir briefly to integrate. Spoke the two brandied cherries
and the twisted-shaved peel of the orange

on a pick and drop into glass. (nix the
fruit and use rye instead of bourbon for a
simpler pre-prohibition version).

OLD FLAME
PDT

2 oz. botanical gin
¾ oz. fresh-squeezed lemon juice
¾ oz. simple syrup
1 egg white

Dry-shake, shake with ice, and strain into
chilled egg coupe. Pour ½ oz. flaming
Green Chartreuse V.E.P. over the surface
of the drink.

OLD 4TH MULE
PDT

1 ½ oz. Old 4th Distillery Vodka
1 oz. House Ginger Beer -or- Fever
  Tree
1 oz. simple syrup
¾ oz. fresh-squeezed lime juice

Shake with ice and strain into a chilled
mule cup filled with ice. Garnish with a
wheel of lime and candied ginger.

THE OPERA
PDT

2 oz. botanical gin
1 oz. Dubonnet Rouge
¼ oz. Mandarin Napolean
1 dash orange bitters

Stir with ice and strain into a chilled
coupe. Garnish with a twist of orange.

PALMER, OLD
FASHIONED
Savoy

1 glass rye whisky
1 dash fresh-squeezed lemon juice

1 dash Angostura bitters

Shake with ice, then strain into an Old-Fashioned glass over a large cube of ice. Garnish with 3 brandied cherries.

PEARMAN'S TODDY

Andrew Baker of Octane Coffee via Old 4th Distillery

2 oz. Old 4th Distillery Gin
1/2 oz. cinnamon simple syrup
1/2 oz. fresh-squeezed lemon juice
7 dashes Angostura bitters

Stir in a heat-proof mug, top with piping hot water; stir well. Garnish with a cinnamon stick.

PERSEPHONE

PDT

1 oz. Laird's Applejack
3/4 oz. Dolin Sweet Vermouth
1/2 oz. Plymouth sloe gin
1/2 oz. fresh-squeezed lemon juice
1/2 oz. **House-made Grenadine** 🗒
1/2 oz. simple syrup
healthy dash of pomegranate juice

Stir with ice and strain into a chilled coupe. Garnish with a handful of pomegranate seeds.

PHILIPPE ☆

Waldorf-Astoria

1/3 oz. green Chartreuse
1/4 oz. Kirschwasser
champagne

Top with champagne!

PINK LADY

PDT

1 1/2 oz. Plymouth Gin
3/4 oz. fresh-squeezed lemon juice

1/2 oz. Laird's Applejack
1/2 oz. simple syrup
1/2 oz. **House-made Grenadine** 🗒
1 egg white

Dry-shake, then shake with ice and strain into a chilled egg coupe.

PISCO SOUR

Victor Vaughen Morris, Lima, 1920s

Served especially on the 1st Saturday of February during the Peruvian public holiday celebrating Pisco!

2 oz. Pisco
3/4 oz. fresh-squeezed lime juice
3/4 oz. simple syrup
1 egg white

Dry-shake (excepting bitters), then shake with ice and fine-strain into a chilled egg coupe. Garnish with 3-4 drops of Angostura Bitters, swirled about in delicate design.

May add 1 oz. St. Germain liqueur and substitute a dash of Orange Bitters for a "Suite Marilyn."

POMPIER

Dietsh

3 oz. dry vermouth
1/2 oz. **Black Currant Shrub** 🗒

Pour together into ice-filled Collins glass, top with soda to taste. Garnish with a lime.

PRINCE OF WALES, 1896 ☆

PDT

1 oz. V.S.O.P. Cognac
1 oz. Madeira
1/4 oz. Grand Mariner
1 dash Angostura bitters
champagne

Stir with ice and strain into a chilled coupe. Top with champagne!

Stir with ice and strain into a chilled coupe. Garnish with an orange twist.

THE PROFESSOR
PDT

2 oz. V.S.O.P. cognac
3/4 oz. Tawny port
1/2 oz. sweet vermouth
1 dash Angostura bitters
1 dash orange bitters

PROHIBITION COCKTAIL
Savoy

1/2 gin
1/2 "Kina Lillet"
1 dash apricot brandy
Splash of fresh orange juice

A FESTIVE AMUSEMENT

THE EPIPHANY TART / TWELFTH CAKES

FROM THE HAWK AND THE OWL, PRIVATE DRINKING HOUSE

- ᗆ On January 6th, into a Kings' Cake (or other type of Epiphany cake) embed a whole clove, a 1-2" twig from a cherry tree, and the clean fragment of a rag.

- ᗆ Whoever finds the hidden Clove is the villain. Whoever finds the hidden Cherry Tree Twig, the fool. Whoever finds the hidden Rag becomes "the tart."

- ᗆ Thus the games begin, as the party goes about helping the three transform into a heroic, wise, and virtuous trio by three rounds of questions and charades from an emptied punch bowl. Serve with ginger snaps and spiced ale -or- scrumptiously-spiced coffee.

- ᗆ Continue playing wholesome practical jokes around the dying embers of the yule log, then chalk your door!

TO EMBARK ON CHALKING THE DOOR:

Write in chalk 20 + C + M + B + 21 In which, CMB stands for "Christus Mansionem Benedicat" (May Christ Bless this House). A Note: in this instance, "21" refers to 2021. In past or future celebrations, "21" would be replaced with the last digits of the new year.

Shake with ice, then strain into a chilled cocktail coupe, add a twist of lemon. Garnish with a lemon peel.

PUMPKIN OLD FASHIONED
18.21 Bitters

2 oz. bourbon
½ oz. 18.21 Pumpkin Spice Shrub
8-10 drops 18.21 Barrel Aged Bitters

Mix and serve over ice.

RAMOS GIN FIZZ
Henry Ramos, New Orleans 1888

1 ½ oz. gin
½ oz. fresh-squeezed lemon juice
½ oz. fresh-squeezed lime juice
½ oz. simple syrup
1 oz. cream
1 egg white
2-3 drops orange flower water

Shake until egg is light and fluffy, then add ice and continue to shake for 2 minutes. Pour 1-2 oz. of soda water into a highball glass, then strain the fizz atop.

QUELLE VIE
(WHAT A LIFE!)
Savoy

⅔ Brandy *to give you courage*
⅓ Kummel *-or-* caraway, cumin, and fennel house-made liqueur *to give you caution*

Shake with ice, then strain into a chilled cocktail glass. Note this cocktail is predominantly courageous and, thus, full of heart! Garnish with a brandied cherry.

RAPSCALLION
PDT

2 ¼ oz. single malt Scotch whisky
¾ oz. Rancho de Philo Triple Cream Sherry

Stir with ice and strain into a chilled coupe, rinsed with St. George Absinthe. Twist a lemon peel over the surface and discard.

RED CARPET REVIVER ☆
Parsons

½ oz. Blood Orange Syrup 🏮
1 oz. Aperol
1 oz. Lillet Blanc
1 dash orange bitters
1 dash grapefruit bitters
champagne

Stir with ice and strain into chilled coupe. Top with champagne! Garnish with a twist of blood orange.

THE REQUIEM
Schmidt

1 oz. brandy
1 dash sherry
1 dash port
1 dash maraschino
1 oz. cream
1 egg
A spoonful of powdered sugar

Shake with ice until egg and cream are light and frothy. Strain into a champagne flute.

RESOLUTE
Savoy

½ dry gin
¼ apricot brandy
¼ juice of fresh-squeezed lemon

Shake with ice, then strain into a chilled cocktail glass. Garnish with a few slices of shaved deeply-frozen hard-crystal ice.

REVEREND PALMER
PDT

2 oz. Black-Tea infused Elijah Craig
   12-yr old bourbon
1/2 oz. lemon syrup
2 dashes Angostura bitters

Stir with ice and strain over one large cube in a chilled rocks glass. Garnish with a twist of lemon.

RICHMOND
Savoy

1/3 Lillet Blanc
2/3 botanical gin
1 tsp. fresh-squeezed lemon juice

Shake with ice, then strain into a chilled cocktail glass. Garnish with a thinly-sliced lemon peel.

ROB ROY
to drink on St. Andrew's Day: Friday, November 30th

1/2 Scotch whisky
1/2 Italian vermouth
1 dash Angostura bitters

Shake with ice, then strain into a chilled cocktail glass. Garnish with a few slices of shaved deeply-frozen hard-crystal ice.

ROMAN HOLIDAY
Waldorf-Astoria

2 oz. Bombay Sapphire Gin
1/2 oz. Aperol
1/2 oz. Cynar
1 oz. fresh blood orange juice

Shake with ice, then strain into a chilled cocktail glass. Garnish with orange peel and a brandied cherry. Best with fresh-squeezed juice.

ROYAL COCKTAIL, NO. 3
Savoy

1/3 botanical gin
1/3 French vermouth
1/3 cherry brandy
1 dash maraschino

Shake with ice, then strain into a chilled cocktail glass. Garnish with a brandied cherry.

ROYAL TENENBAUM
Stewart

1 1/2 oz. London dry gin
1/2 oz. Alsatian pine liqueur *(bourgeon de sapin)*, such as Zirbenz Stone Pine Liqueur
1 sprig fresh rosemary

Shake the gin and pine liqueur over ice, strain into a cocktail glass. Garnish with a sprig of rosemary.

RUBY
Waldorf-Astoria

2 oz. Rothman & Winter orchard cherry liqueur
1 oz. Noilly Prat extra dry vermouth and 5 dashes Horsford's acid phosphate
 -or- sweet vermouth, to preference
1/4 oz. Luxardo maraschino liqueur
2 dashes Regans' orange bitters No.6

Stir with ice until chilled, then strain into a chilled cocktail glass. Garnish with a lemon peel.

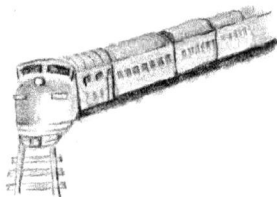

RUBY FIZZ
Tasty n' Sons, 2011

1 oz. Plymouth sloe gin
1 oz. Plymouth Gin
1 egg white
1/4 oz. fresh-squeezed lemon juice
1 oz. **House-made Grenadine** 🍸

Dry-shake until egg is light and frothy, then shake with ice for 30 seconds or until chilled; strain into a chilled cocktail glass; top with club soda. Garnish with a few drops of seasonal bitters.

RUN RUN RUDOLPH
the Miracle Bar, Atlanta

2 oz. Blanco Tequila
1 oz. coffee Liqueur
1 oz. **Iced Hot Chocolate** 🍸
Dash of "Mexican Spices"

Shake with ice, then strain into a chilled cocktail glass.

RUSTY NAIL, 1937
Savoy, David Wondrich

1 1/2 -2 oz. **Scotch whisky** -or- *Applejack for a New Amsterdam*
1/2 - 3/4 oz. Drambuie

Shake whisky with ice, then strain into an old-fashioned glass, float Drambuie on top. Serve on the rocks, neat, or up. Garnish with a lemon peel.

RUSSIAN GRAND DUKE
Waldorf-Astoria

Prohibition-era cocktail with alternate variations included

2 oz. Russian Standard vodka -or- VSOP cognac
1 oz. fresh-squeezed lemon juice
1/2 oz. simple syrup -or- house-made grenadine -or- house-made raspberry syrup
1/4 oz. Original Recipe absinthe -or- Bénédictine
1 dash Regan's Orange Bitters No. 6 -or- house-made cranberry bitters

Shake with ice and a few dashes of lemon juice, then strain into a chilled cocktail glass. Garnish with a lemon peel.

SAGE OLD BUCK
PDT

1/2 oz. single malt Scotch whisky
3/4 oz. fresh-squeezed lemon juice
3/4 oz. house-made Ginger Beer
 -or- **Fever Tree** *spiced orange ginger ale*
 -or- *ginger beer*
3/4 oz. simple syrup
1/2 oz. Belle de Brillet
1/4 oz. Vanilla
8 whole black peppercorns

Muddle the black peppercorns with the simple syrup. Add everything else, then shake with ice and fine-strain into a chilled Collins glass filled with ice. Garnish with a gently-slapped leaf of sage.

SAKÉ TODDY
The Hawk and the Owl

6 oz. saké
1 oz. genever
1/2 oz. green Chartreuse
1/2 oz. maraschino liqueur
1/4 oz. ginger liqueur -or- freshly squeezed juice of ginger
1/4 oz. agave -or- local honey
1/4 tsp. absinthe
squeeze of lemon, to taste

Heat the sake in a bain-marie (do not bring to a boil).

Pour the sake and everything else into a

preheated heat-proof mug. Garnish with a lemon wheel studded with 6 cloves. Spear 2 maraschino cherries for a festive finish

SPANISH G&T
18.21 Bitters

2 oz. botanical gin
4-5 oz. 18.21 Tonic
18.21 Tart Cherry + Saffron Bitters

Served over ice in a balloon wine glass. Garnish with sprigs of thyme, a lemon slice, and whole allspice

SPICED WINTER PALOMA
18.21 Bitters

2 oz. best tequila
½ oz. Cocchi Rosa
½ oz. 18.21 Blood Orange + Ginger Shrub
½ oz. grapefruit juice
8-10 drops 18.21 Japanese Chili + Lime Bitters

Mix and serve over ice.

ST. GERMAIN
Savoy

½ lemon, freshly-juiced
¼ grapefruit, freshly-juiced
1 egg white
4 oz. green Chartreuse

Dry-shake until egg is light and frothy, add ice, then continue to shake until chilled. Strain into a chilled cocktail glass, with a dash of preferred bitters atop the egg white.

SAVANNAH
Waldorf-Astoria

2 oz. Plymouth Gin
1 oz. fresh-squeezed orange juice
¼ oz. Tempus Fugit crème de cacao
½ egg white

Dry-shake until egg white is light and fluffy, then add ice and shake. Fine-strain into a chilled cocktail glass. Garnish with orange peel.

SAVOY TANGO
Savoy

½ sloe gin
½ Applejack -or- Calvados

Shake with ice, then strain into a chilled cocktail glass. Garnish with a brandied cherry, and leave a path to an open dance floor.

SEELBACH, 1917 LOUISVILLE ☆
PDT, Parsons

1 oz. pre-prohibition style bourbon
½ oz. Cointreau
3 dashes Peychaud's Bitters
2 dashes Angostura bitters
champagne

Stir with ice and strain into a chilled coupe. Top with champagne! Garnish with a twist of orange.

SIDECAR
PDT

2 oz. V.S.O.P. Cognac
¾ oz. Cointreau
¾ oz. fresh-squeezed lemon juice
¼ oz. simple syrup

Shake with ice and strain into a chilled, sugared-rim coupe.

SIDEKICK
Tasty n' Sons, 2011

1 oz. Clear Creek Pear Brandy
1 oz. Combier d'Orange
A few dashes Allspice Dram
¼ oz. fresh-squeezed lemon juice

Shake with ice, then strain into a sugared-rim brandy snifter. Garnish with a slice of orange.

SILVER SANGAREE
PDT

1 ½ oz. Paumanok Cabernet Franc
¾ oz. fresh-squeezed lemon juice
½ oz. blended Scotch whisky
½ oz. Ruby port
½ oz. **Clove Syrup** 🔖
4 Kirsch Brandied-Cherries
1 egg white

Add the cherries and clove syrup to a mixing glass and muddle. Add everything else then dry-shake. Shake with ice and strain into a chilled wine glass. Garnish with grated nutmeg.

SIMPLY WAITING FOR SANTA, NO. 1
the Miracle Bar, Atlanta

Cinnamon-infused bourbon over a snowball rock, i.e., large sphere of ice.

SIMPLY WAITING FOR SANTA, NO. 2
the Miracle Bar, Atlanta

Gingerbread-spiced rye over a snowball rock, i.e., large sphere of ice.

SINGLE MALT SANGAREE
PDT

2 oz. Paumanok Cabernet Franc
1 oz. 14-yr old single malt Scotch whisky
1 oz. Dubonnet
¾ oz. Grand Mariner
1 tsp. Demerara syrup

Heat until steaming. Pour into preheated heat-proof mug. Twist an orange peel over the surface and discard. Garnish with a cinnamon stick.

SING SING
Dietsh

1 oz. apple brandy
1 oz. St. George Terroir Gin
½ oz. **Apple-Cardamom Shrub** 🔖
 -or- Cinnamon Apple Shrub excl. spice
½ oz. fresh-squeezed lemon juice
¼ oz. **House-made Grenadine** 🔖
¼ oz. Bittermans Citron Sauvage
4-5 dashes of Peychaud's Bitters

Shake with ice, then strain into an Old Fashioned glass.

> "At Christmas play and make good cheer,
> For Christmas comes but once a year."
>
> —THOMAS TUSSER, 1557

SIR DUKE
Venkman's

1 oz. house-made basil-infused vodka
½ oz. Chartreuse
½ oz. Luxardo Maraschino
½ oz. fresh-squeezed lime

Shake well with ice, then strain into a cocktail glass. Garnish with thin slice of lime.

SNOWBALL
Savoy

⅙ crème de violette
⅙ crème de menthe
⅙ Anisette
⅙ sweet cream
⅓ dry gin

Shake with ice, then strain into a chilled cocktail glass. Garnish with a thinly sliced half-wedge of grapefruit.

THE SNOWBALL
Schmidt

1 egg
1 spoonful powdered sugar
1 bottle of authentic house-made ginger ale
1 oz. brandy

Beat egg with sugar until light and frothy, add the brandy and shake until incorporated. Pour ice-cold ginger ale over tall tall ice-filled collins glass.

SNOWBALL FIZZ
Waldorf-Astoria

2 oz. rum
½ oz. simple syrup
½ egg white
2 oz. chilled Feverfew Ginger Ale

Dry-shake all ingredients (save the ginger ale) until egg white is light and fluffy. Add ice then shake until chilled. Strain into a Collins glass, then top with ginger ale, lightly stir to incorporate.

SNOWBALL OLD-FASHIONED
the Miracle Bar, Atlanta

2 oz. **Gingerbread Bourbon** 🥃
Dash Wormwood Bitters
¼ oz. fresh-squeezed lemon juice

Shake with ice then strain into an Old Fashioned glass with one large cube or sphere of ice. Garnish with 2 brandied cherries.

SOLSTICE
PDT

1 ½ oz. Bonded Rye Whisky
½ oz. Laird's Bonded Apple Brandy
½ oz. Nonino Amaro
½ oz. Dubonnet Rouge
¼ oz. **House-made Grenadine** 🥃

Stir with ice and strain into a chilled coupe.

THIS SOUTHERN-INSPIRED SORGHUM FLIP
Parsons

2 oz. bourbon
½ oz. buttermilk
1 egg
3 tbsp. Georgia pecans *chopped, toasted*
Pinch of cinnamon
1 tsp. brown sugar
1 tbsp. sorghum syrup *-or-* molasses
2 dashes house-made Coffee-Pecan Bitters *-or-* Fee Brothers Whiskey Barrel Aged Bitters

Dry-shake until egg is well-incorporated, then shake with ice. Double-strain into a chilled old-fashioned glass. Garnish with freshly-grated nutmeg.

STAR OF BETHLEHEM
The Hawk and the Owl

1 oz. best botanical gin
1 oz. vermouth, to preference
1 1/2 oz. white port
1 tsp. anise-liqueur
2 oz. fresh-squeezed mandarin juice
1 egg white

Dry-shake all but gin, until light and frothy, add gin, then stir with ice, then strain into a chilled cocktail glass. Garnish with an anise star and 3 dashes of seasonal bitters.

THE STAR NATION COSMOS
Starvation Alley Cranberry Juice Co.

4 parts vodka
1/2 part Starvation Alley Cranberry Juice
1 part simple syrup
1 part applejack brandy
1 part lime juice

Shake with ice, and pour over a large cube of ice. Garnish with an orange twist.

STAR NATION NEGRONI
Starvation Alley Cranberry Juice Co.

recipe developed at Pickled Fish, Long Beach, Washington

1 part Starvation Alley Cranberry Juice
1 part sweet vermouth
1 part gin

Shake with ice, and pour over a large cube of ice. Run an orange twist around the rim

and toss into the glass.

STRATOSPHERE ☆
The Stork Club, 1946

4-6 oz. champagne *(recommended: brut)*
3/4 - 1 oz. deeply-chilled Crème de Yvette
Thin slice of lemon to twist
2 cloves

Pour deeply-chilled chilled Crème de Yvette into a tall-stemmed champagne flute, top with champagne! Twist a lemon for juice on top, then discard. Garnish with 2 pieces of clove. Serve very cold.

SUGAR PLUM FAIRY FLIP
The Hawk and the Owl

2 oz. favorite bourbon
1 oz. Clear Creek Plum Brandy
1/2 oz. fresh-squeezed lemon juice
1 egg
1/2 tbsp. powdered sugar
2 dashes bitters, of choice
Pinch of cinnamon
1 sugared plum

Dry-shake until egg is light and frothy, then shake with ice until chilled. Strain into an old-fashioned glass. Garnish with a sprinkling of cinnamon and a sugared-plum and 2 brandied-cherries on a pick.

THE SVELTE ROSE
Another "Jim Beach Mystery?"

1 oz. Bulleit rye
1 oz. Death's Door gin
1/2 oz. Aalborg akvavit
1/2 oz. Horton port
1/2 oz. fresh-squeezed lemon

Stir in a mixing glass until incorporated, then strain into a chilled martini glass. Garnish with freshly-grated nutmeg.

SWISS MIST
PDT

2 oz. Plymouth Gin
3/4 oz. fresh-squeezed lemon juice
3/4 oz. grapefruit syrup
1 egg white

Dry-shake, then shake with ice and strain into a chilled egg coupe. Garnish with a spritz of Kubler Absinthe.

TO MAKE: GRAPEFRUIT SYRUP

24 oz. simple syrup
3 Southern grapefruits

Using a microplane, remove zest from grapefruits. Combine grapefruit zest with simple syrup in a non-reactive container. Infuse for 10 minutes at room temperature. Fine-strain, bottle, and store in the refrigerator.

SYMPHONY OF MOIST JOY
Waldorf-Astoria

1/2 oz. Combier Rose liqueur
1/2 oz. Chartreuse
1/2 oz. Tempus Fugit crème de cacao
 -or- crème de menthe
1/2 Hennessy VS cognac

Add shaved ice to a coupe or small wine-glass, pour ingredients in order listed above. Garnish with seasonal bitters and fresh mint (optional).

THE TERMINUS
The Hawk and the Owl

an Iconic New Year's Eve Atlantan Flip

2-3 oz. Four Roses, Old 4th, -or- Bainbridge Distillery's Bourbon Whiskey
1/2 - 1 oz. heavy cream
1/4 oz. simple syrup
1 egg
2 dashes of 18.21 Earl Grey bitters

3/4 - 2 oz. Kopke Tawny port

Dry-shake egg, cream, and simple syrup until egg is light and frothy, then add the spirits, shake with ice, and strain into a chilled goblet containing the bitters. Garnish with freshly-grated nutmeg. Toast to the city; drink while overlooking the winter sky -or- skyline.

TOM AND JERRY
Jerry Thomas, Waldorf-Astoria,
Old Mr. Boston

A traditional Christmas classic

2 cups. sugar
12 eggs, at room temperature to be
 separated: whites and yolks
1 1/2 tsp. ground cinnamon
1/2 tsp. cloves
1/2 tsp. allspice
1/2 tsp. vanilla extract
1 pint Jamaican rum
1 pint brandy

Beat the whites of the eggs to a stiff froth, adding half amount of sugar; then (in a separate bowl) beat the yolks until they pale yellow and thoroughly blended, thicken with remaining amount of sugar until the mixture attains the smooth consistency of light batter, add vanilla, then the spices. Carefully fold the egg whites (meringues) into the yolk mixture. {note: this cocktail is often pre-mixed (without the spirits) as a "batter," and kept in a bottle from which a wine-glassful is used to prepare each tumler of "Tom and Jerry."}

Take a small bar glass, and to one tablespoonful of the above mixture, add one wine-glass full of spirits, and fill the heat-proof glass with piping hot water, grate fresh nutmeg on top. The secret to a good Tom and Jerry is a stiff batter and a warm mug.

TURKEY SHOOT
Parsons

1 ½ oz. high-proof rye
½ oz. Punt e Mes
¼ oz. St. Elizabeth Allspice Dram
¾ oz. cinnamon syrup
¼ oz. fresh-squeezed lemon juice
1 dash Fee Brothers Whiskey Barrel-Aged Bitters
1 dash cranberry bitters

Shake with ice until chilled. Strain into a chilled old-fashioned glass over one large cube of ice. Garnish with a thick piece of lemon zest.

TO MAKE: CIDER REDUCTION

In a small saucepan, bring 1 cup of local apple cider to a boil and cook until the liquid is reduced to half (about 30 minutes). Allow to cool before using. May store in the refrigerator for up to a week.

TO MAKE: CINNAMON SYRUP

In a medium saucepan, combine 1 cup of water, 1 cup of organic fair-trade sugar, and 4 cinnamon stick. Bring to a simmer, stirring occasionally to dissolve the sugar. At the first crack of a boil, remove from heat. Once cooled, remove the cinnamon sticks and store the syrup in a glass jar in the refrigerator up to 1 month.

> "Christmas is here,
> Merry old Christmas,
> Gift-bearing, heart-touching,
> joy-bringing Christmas,
> Day of grand memories,
> king of the year."
>
> –WASHINGTON
> IRVING

TUXEDO
PDT, Waldorf-Astoria, classic

2 oz. Plymouth Gin
1 ½ oz. Dolin Dry Vermouth
¼ oz. Luxardo Maraschino Liqueur
2 dashes orange bitters

Stir with ice and strain into a chilled coupe, having first rinsed it with Vieux Pontarlier Absinthe. Garnish with a twist of lemon and a cherry.

You may choose to substitute 1 oz. Lustau Manzanilla or amontillado sherry for the Vermouth and Maraschino, for a simpler achievement

ULTRAMODERN
Dietsh

2 oz. favorite bourbon
½ oz. smoky scotch *i.e. Laphroaig*
½ oz. **Fig-Cinnamon Shrub** 🏺
2 dashes Angostura bitters

Shake with ice, then double-strain into a rocks glass containing one large ice cube or sphere. Garnish with whatever calls to you..

UP TO DATE
PDT

2 oz. Rye Whisky
¾ oz. Lustau Mansanilla *-or-* Oloroso Sherry
½ oz. Grand Marnier
2 dashes Angostura bitters

Stir with ice and strain into a chilled coupe. Garnish with a twist of lemon.

VALENCIA ☆
Johnnie Hansen, 1927

1 ½ oz. Rothman & Winter Orchard Apricot Liqueur *-or-* Apricot Brandy

¾ oz. fresh-squeezed orange juice
4 dashes orange bitters -or- Angostura bitters
1 oz. Armagnac *optional*
Bit of bubbly

Shake, then strain into chilled highball glass, and top with champagne! Garnish with an orange peel.

THE VELVET GLOVE CLUB ☆
PDT

1 oz. Hine V.S.O.P. Cognac
½ oz. Lillet Blanc
½ oz. Marie Brizard White crème de cacao
champagne

Stir with ice and strain into a chilled coupe. Top with champagne!

VERTE CHAUD
French Alps, ski villages

Best hot chocolate
1 tsp. of Green Chartreuse

Add Green Chartreuse to the best HOT chocolate, stir with wooden spoon. Serve piping hot for magnificent apres ski experience.

VESPERS
The Hawk and the Owl

To be served at -or- after the sunset, and to be accompanied by candleglow and evensong

1 oz. Chartreuse
1 oz. botanical gin
½ oz. Plum Eau de Vie
¼ oz. Clear Creek Douglas Fir Eau de Vie
1" vanilla bean seeds, scraped
1 tsp. fresh-squeezed lemon juice
1 dash of elecampane bitters *optional*

Shake with ice, then strain into a chilled cocktail glass. Garnish with a thinly-sliced lemon peel and 2 brandied cherries. Serve with 2 pieces fresh marzipan sprinkled with a hint of spice.

VIEUX CARRE, 1938 NEW ORLEANS
PDT, Parsons, Waldorf-Astoria

1 oz. Straight Rye Whisky
1 oz. Hine V.S.O.P. Cognac
1 oz. Carpano Antica Sweet Vermouth
¼ oz. Bénédictine
1 dash Angostura bitters
1-2 dashes Peychaud's Bitters

Stir with ice and strain over one large cube into a chilled rocks glass. Garnish with a twist of lemon.

VIRGIN
Savoy

⅓ Jacquin's Forbidden Fruit liqueur
 -or- similar liqueur, if unavailable.
⅓ white crème de menthe
⅓ high-quality dry gin

Stir well, then strain into an elegant glass appropriate for the occasion.

WALK IN THE WOODS
Waldorf-Astoria

1-2 oz. Buffalo Trace Bourbon
½ - 1 oz. Sandeman Fine Rich Madeira
1 oz. fresh local apple cider
¾ oz. fresh-squeezed lemon juice
¼ oz. grade B Lamb Sugarworks Dark Robust maple syrup
1 dash Angostura bitters

Shake with ice, then strain into a chilled cocktail glass. Garnish with freshly-grated nutmeg.

WARD EIGHT
PDT

2 oz. Rye Whisky
½ oz. fresh-squeezed lemon juice
½ oz. fresh-squeezed orange juice
¼ oz. simple syrup
1 tsp. Pomegranate Molasses

Shake with ice and strain into a chilled coupe.

WE KINGS THREE
The Hawk and the Owl

2 oz. best rum
1 oz. peppermint
1 oz. best chocolate, melted
1 oz. Goldschläger *(cinnamon schnapps)* over a Snowball Rock of ice
1 dash Myrrh tincture

Light Frankincense (away from direct flow), to set atmosphere as you build this cocktail. Shake with ice, then strain into chilled cocktail glass. Garnish with a brandied cherry.

WELCOME STRANGER
Savoy

⅙ House-made Grenadine 🍶
⅙ fresh-squeezed lemon juice
⅙ fresh-squeezed orange juice
⅙ botanical gin
⅙ Swedish punch
⅙ best brandy

Shake with ice, then strain into a chilled cocktail glass. Garnish with thin slices of orange and lemon.

WELLINGTON FLIP
PDT

2 oz. vodka
1 oz. heavy cream
1 kiwi

1 passionfruit
¾ oz. fresh-squeezed lime juice
½ oz. Kassatly Chtaura Orgeat
1 egg white

Puree kiwi and passionfruit, add orgeat, then other ingredients and dry-shake until smooth and frothy, then shake with ice and strain into a chilled Collins glass. Garnish with 3 spritzes diluted Aftel Bergamot Essence.

WELLNESS TODDY
The Hawk and the Owl

2-3 oz. Makers' Mark *-or-* bourbon of choice
1 tbsp. local honey
¼ fresh-squeezed lemon juice
¼" freshly-grated ginger
Pinch of cayenne *optional*

Top with piping hot water, stir. Serve with a spoon. Toast "to your good health" and enjoy!

WHEN BOURBON WAS KING
PDT

2 oz. bourbon
¾ oz. Godiva Original Liqueur
¾ oz. fresh juice of a blood orange

Shake with ice and strain over a chilled coupe. Garnish with a flamed orange twist. Best with fresh-squeezed juice.

WHISKY SOUR
classic

Juice of ½ lemon *about ¾ oz.*
½ tbsp. sugar *-or- ½ oz. simple syrup*
1 glass *(-or- about 2 oz.)* of preferred
   whiskey *brandy, genever, gin, rum...*
½ egg white *optional*

Shake well with ice until sugar is dissolved,
then strain into footed sours glass with
one squirt of soda water. Garnish with a
slice of orange and a brandied cherry.

WHIST
Savoy, Schmidt

*2 classic pre-prohibition variations sharing the
same name but vastly different.*

¼ best rum
¼ Italian vermouth
½ Calvados

Shake with ice, then strain into a chilled
cocktail glass.

-or, alternatively-

Steep 1 oz. of Orange Pekoe tea in 1 qt. of
having-been-boiled water. Strain out the
tea leaves with a sieve, then dissolve 1 lb.
of organic sugar, the juice of 5-6 lemons,
and mix with 1750mL bottle of Bordeaux.
Heat without bringing to a boil, then serve
into heat-proof glasses or ceramic mugs.

WHISPERS OF
THE FROST
Waldorf-Astoria

1 oz. rye whiskey
1 oz. tawny *-or-* ruby port
1 oz. Lustau Don Nino oloroso sherry
   oz. house-made Demerara syrup
2 dashes Angostura bitters *optional*

Stir with ice, then strain into goblet or Old
Fashioned glass over large ice cubes or

spheres. Garnish with seasonal fruit.

*For a warmer cold-winter-night variety, add a
½ oz. of hot water and a stick of cinnamon.*

WHITE BIRCH FIZZ
PDT

1 ½ oz. Plymouth Gin
¾ oz. fresh-squeezed lemon juice
½ oz. Strega
½ oz. Rothman & Winter Orchard
   Apricot
1 egg white
Spitz of club soda
Spritz of Suze liqueur

Dry-shake, then shake with ice. Strain
into a chilled Collins glass. Top with Club
Soda and garnish with a spritz of Suze.

THE WHISPER MOUSE
The Hawk and the Owl

Inspired by DIY Bitters

2 oz. best fruit-infused cognac *-or-*
   Lillet
1 tbsp. Hazelnut Hearth Bitters {*see
   below*}
Dash of Lamb Sugarworks Dark
   Robust maple syrup, to taste

Shake with ice, then strain into lovely
cocktail glass.

TO MAKE: HAZELNUT
HEARTH BITTERS

½ oz. fresh-squeezed lemon juice,
   strained
½ oz. pure Lamb Sugarworks Dark
   Robust maple syrup
3 oz. hazelnut tincture
2 oz. birch bark tincture *-or-* winter-
   green tincture
1 oz. andrographis tincture
1 tsp. cayenne tincture

Combine in an 8 oz. amber dropper bottle.

WINTER
Waldorf-Astoria

2 oz. Jamaican dark rum
½ oz. fresh-squeezed lime juice
½ oz. simple syrup
¼ oz. The Bitter Truth pimento dram
  -or- St. Elizabeth allspice dram
1 dash Angostura bitters

Shake with ice, then strain into a chilled
cocktail glass. Garnish with orange peel.

WINTER'S NAP
Waldorf-Astoria

1 ½ oz. botanical gin -or- preferred
  vodka
1 oz. Cocchi Americano
1 oz. Aperol

Stir with ice in mixing glass, then strain
into Old-Fashioned glass filled with large
ice cubes or spheres. Garnish with a
rosemary twig, gently handled to release
essence.

WINTER SOLSTICE FLOAT
Zachos

2 oz. rye whiskey
1 oz. **Celtic Nocino** 🍶
2 tsp. - 1 cup vanilla ice-cream with
  about a tsp. either spicebush,
  cinnamon, -or- allspice folded in on
  cutting board.

Shake the rye and the nocino with ice,
then strain into ice-cream goblet. Top with
a scoop of spicebush ice-cream.

THE WOODLAND MARC DE CHAMPAGNE ☆
The Hawk and the Owl

1 oz. Art in the Age Root Liqueur
1 oz. Nocino
2 oz. Fortified wine
2 oz. Marc de Champagne

Shake with ice, then strain into a chilled
cocktail glass. Top with champagne.
Garnish with a brandied cherry.

WONDRICH
PDT

2 oz. Jameson 12-yr old Irish Whisky
¾ oz. Lillet Blanc
½ Cointreau
2 dashes orange bitters

Stir with ice and strain into a chilled
coupe. Garnish with a twist of orange.

WOOLWORTH
PDT

2 oz. blended Scotch whisky
1 oz. Rancho de Philo Triple Cream
  Sherry
½ oz. Bénédictine
2 dashes orange bitters

Stir with ice and strain into a chilled coupe.

"**Success.** Four flights Thursday morning.
All against twenty-one-mile wind. Started from level with engine
power alone. Average speed through air thirty-one miles. Longest
fifty-nine seconds. Inform press. Home Christmas."

- WILBUR AND ORVILLE WRIGHT, DECEMBER 17, 1903

XERXES
Savoy

Seasonal ode to Jake Pflaum

6 oz. Triple Cream Sherry
Dash of orange bitters
Dash of peach bitters

Stir in a mixing glass with ice, then strain
into a chilled sherry glass.

X MARKS THE SPOT
Waldorf-Astoria

1 ½ oz. Appleton Estate white rum
½ oz. Gifford Banane du Bresil
   liqueur
½ oz. Domaine de Canton ginger
   liqueur
½ oz. fresh-squeezed lime juice
½ oz. fresh-squeezed orange juice
½ egg white
1 dash pimento bitters

Dry-shake until egg is light and fluffy
and ingredients are well-incorporated,
add ice, and continue to shake. Then,
fine-strain into chilled cocktail glass. *Float
a barspoon or two of ruby port on surface.
Garnish with one star anise, also on surface.*

YULETIDE
OLD-FASHIONED
Waldorf-Astoria

1 Demerara sugar cube
3 dashes Dale DeGroff's pimento bitters *-or-* St. Elizabeth allspice dram
2 ½ oz. Apple, Pear, and Orange
   Peel-infused Bourbon 🕮
1 large swath lemon peel

Add sugar cube to Old Fashioned glass.
Muddle to dissolve and incorporate sugar.
Add whiskey and stir, insuring sugar is
dissolved and well-distributed. Add ice and
stir briefly to chill. Garnish with lemon peel.

1860 MANHATTAN
Waldorf-Astoria

2 oz. 12-yr. old single-barrel bourbon
1 oz. sweet vermouth
¼ oz. dry curaçao *-or-* Luxardo maraschino liqueur
2 dashes Angostura bitters

Stir with ice, then strain into a chilled
cocktail glass. Garnish with three delicious brandied-cherries.

5 STAR
Waldorf-Astoria

2 oz. Pirate xo rum
½ oz. Dark Robust maple syrup
1 oz. half-and-half *-or-* milk
1 healthy pinch authentic Chinese
   five-spice powder

Shake all but the Chinese Five Spice with
ice. Fine-strain into chilled Old Fashioned
glass. Garnish with a pinch of spice
delicately sprinkled in the center.

PUNCHES, BOWLS, GROG, NEGUS, MULLED WINES AND CIDERS

Most of the recipes found herein are of such timeless classics, that few can claim to know their true origin. Thus, in most instances I have left these heirlooms as I originally found them, without edits, despite their archaic language. I have noted from whom I discovered these antiquated gems in the hopes that over a lifetime, I, too, may unmask and learn of their contributions to our modern Christmas story. Much of these can be found within the "public domain," such as any of the recipes below attributed to Jerry Thomas, Savoy, or Schmidt. As their legatees and heirs, it is my hope, that reprinting them here now, in this compendium, that you, too, will be inspired to test them, improve upon them, serve them, and revitalize such treasures of the "communal bowl" that Christmas best calls forth into being.

BASIC PUNCH RECIPE
Waldorf-Astoria

1 bottle spirit of choice *winter = cognac*
6-8 oz. fresh-squeezed lemon juice
½ portion **Oleo Saccharum** 🍸
1 qt. block of ice

Combine all ingredients a few hours prior, then refrigerate until guests are expected to arrive. Then add to block of ice and punch bowl. Garnish with freshly-grated nutmeg.

BASS WYATT
Savoy

4 glasses dry gin
⅔ glass cherry brandy *-or-* curacao
⅓ glass of fresh lemon juice
4 dashes orange bitters
½ tbsp. powdered sugar
1 tbsp. vanilla extract
4 eggs

Beat the eggs until broken, light, and frothy. Add the other ingredients, stirring with ice until well-incorporated and chilled, but without bruising the gin. Double strain into 5 glasses with frosted rims of lemon and sugar. Garnish with freshly-grated nutmeg.

BRANDY CIDER NECTAR PUNCH
Waldorf-Astoria

32 oz. J.K. Scrumpy's *-or-* any preferred hard apple dry cider
10 oz. sparkling water
3 oz. Hennessy VS cognac
2 oz. Lustau Don Nuno oloroso sherry
2 oz. fresh-squeezed lemon juice
¼ portion **Oleo Saccharum** 🍸
Several large ice cubes
Freshly-grated nutmeg for garnish

Serve from a pitcher, or double this recipe and serve from a bowl with dried apple slices.

BRANDY MILK PUNCH
Dave Wondrich via The Bitter Southerner

2 tsp. superfine sugar
2 tsp. water
1 oz. Santa Cruz rum
2 oz. cognac
1 ½ oz. milk
may add, ½ tsp. vanilla extract
  -or- hazelnut/ nutty liqueur for a
  modern twist

Fill half-a-tumbler with shaved -or-
crushed ice. Shake well until milk is frothy.
Strain into a chilled odd-fashioned glass.
Garnish with freshly-grated nutmeg and
serve on a silver tray with a side of ginger
molasses cookies, or to preference.

CHAMPAGNE PUNCH ☆
Jerry Thomas, Waldorf-Astoria

1 quart bottle of wine
¼ lb. sugar
1 orange sliced
The juice of one lemon
3 slices of pineapple
1 wine glass of raspberry -or-
  strawberry syrup
*Ornament with fruits in season, and serve in
champagne goblets.*

This can be made in any quantity by
observing the proportions of the ingredients
as given above. Four bottles of wine make
a gallon, and a gallon is generally sufficient
for fifteen persons in a mixed party .

"CHARMED, SIMPLY CHARMED."
the "Almond," Savoy

Slightly warm 2 glasses of good gin. Add
a teaspoonful of organic powdered sugar.
In this, soak 6 peeled almonds and a
crushed Georgia peach pit, stir until sugar

is dissolved, then allow mixture to cool
to room temperature. Refrigerate until
cold. Once cold, add 2 tablespoons of
Kirsh, 1 tablespoon of best-crafted Peach
Brandy, a glass of French Vermouth, and
2 glasses of high-quality sweet white wine.
Stir vigorously until all is well-incorporated.
Ladle out into a mixing glass, each serving
of 6, shake with ice, then serve up in chilled
wine glasses.

Serve with 2 amaretti cookies.

CIDER PUNCH
Jerry Thomas

On the thin rind of half a lemon pour half
a pint of sherry; add a quarter of a pound
of sugar, the juice of a lemon, a little
grated nutmeg, and a bottle of cider; mix
it well, and, if possible, place it in ice. Add,
before serving, a glass of brandy, and a
few pieces of cucumber rind.

CONFESSION OF LOVE, NO. 342
Schmidt

Infuse ½ oz. of fine black tea in ½ pint of
boiling water for 5 minutes; decant and
pour into a tureen, rub the rind of a lemon
on 3 lbs. of lump-sugar; refine in 1 pint
of boiling water; skim well, add a piece
of vanilla bean, cut into small pieces,
and ½ of dried orange flowers, take the
sugar from the fire, and leave the vanilla
and orange flowers in it for 1 hour. Then,
strain through a sieve into a tureen, Add
a wineglass of maraschino and the juice
of 5 oranges, 2 bottles of Rhine wine, 2
bottles of Medoc, 1 bottle of Madeira,
and 1 bottle of arrack, let the mixture get
very hot without coming to a boil. Serve
piping hot.

DIXIE WHISKY
Savoy

To 2 lumps of organic fair-trade sugar add a small teaspoon of Angostura Bitters, another teaspoon of fresh-squeezed lemon juice, 4 glasses of whisky, a small teaspoon of Curacao, and 2 teaspoons of creme de menthe. Shake with plenty of ice, then strain into 6 cocktail glasses.

ENGLISH BURNED PUNCH
Schmidt

Rub the rind of 3 lemons lightly on one lb. of sugar, put the sugar in an earthen pot, and pour over it 1qt. of rum and 1qt. of claret; stir all together well over fire (gas flame will do splendidly) until it begins to boil and sugar is dissolved; add 1 qt. of good water and the juice of your 3 lemons. Serve hot. Garnish with wintry spices, to preference.

ENGLISH CLARET PUNCH
Schmidt

Boil, in half a pint of water, ½ lb. organic lump-sugar with ⅛ oz. cinnamon, 1/10 oz. ground cinnamon, a few pulverized cloves, and the thinly-peeled rind of an orange, stirring frequently with a wooden spoon until it becomes sort of a syrup. Add 2 750mL bottles of claret. Remove from heat before it's brought back near to boil. Serve warm with a fresh-slice of orange and garnish, to preference.

ENGLISH PUNCH
Schmidt

Rub the rind of 3 lemons lightly on one

lb. of sugar, put the sugar in a tureen, squeeze the juice of your 3 lemons into it and add 1 qt. of good water, add 3 gills of rum and 1 qt. of your best brandy into it and stir continuously over fire (gas flame will do splendidly) until it sugar is dissolved; and. Serve hot. Garnish with freshly-grated nutmeg.

FLYING SCOTCHMAN
Savoy

2 ½ glasses Italian vermouth
3 glasses Scotch whisky
1 tbsp. bitters, to taste
1 tbsp. simple syrup

Shake with ice, then equally strain into 6 cocktail glasses.

GEORGE IV PUNCH ☆
Schmidt

On 7 oz. of sugar rub the peel of 2 organic lemons and 2 bitter (Seville) oranges, put into a tureen with the juice of the fruits and let sit for an hour while you go about other good work. Add 1 cup of boiling water and stir until sugar is thoroughly dissolved. Add 1 pint of perfectly-steeped green tea, ½ pint of freshly-juiced pineapple, 8 oz. of maraschino liqueur, 4 tablespoons of best arrack, and 1 pint of best brandy. Mix well, allow to cool. Serve on ice in champagne flutes, top with champagne. Garnish with a poppy blossom.

GLÖGG

Traditional popular Norwegian holiday drink

1 pound golden raisins
1 ²/₃ cups; ½ cup + 1 tbsp. sugar
60 cardamom pods, broken with
  mortar and pestle
8 cinnamon sticks
12 whole cloves
2 bottles brandy
4 bottles port
2 tsps almond extract

Place the raisins, first portion of sugar, and spices into a square of cheesecloth and bring together the edges and tie off to form a spice bag, then put in a large kettle with enough water to cover. Bring the water to a boil, then reduce heat and simmer for 1 hour. Remove bag, discard, and add the spirits.

Melt the 2nd portion of sugar over a low flame, then once caramelized, mix well into the concoction. With a lighted match, carefully ignite the glögg and allow to burn for about 7 seconds, Cover with pan until flames subside. Allow to cool thoroughly, then store in refrigerator. Serve warm or at room temperature.

GREAT SMOKY MOUNTAIN PUNCH ☆

Jerry Thomas

5 bottles of champagne
1 quart Jamaican rum
1 pint maraschino
6 lemons, sliced
Sugar to taste

Mlx the above ingredients in a large punch-bowl, then place in the center of the bowl a large square block of ice, ornamented on top with rock candy, loaf-sugar, sliced lemons or oranges, pomegranates or fruits of the season. This is a splendid punch for New Year's Day.

HIPPOCRAS BOWL, NO. 451

Schmidt

A kind of spiced wine during the medieval age, a recipe for concocting hippocras, which Talleyraut, the head cook for Charles VII, King of France, has made reads as follows: To a quart of wine, take ⅓ oz. of fine cinnamon, ⅛ oz. of ginger, ¼ oz. cloves, ¼ oz. freshly-grated nutmeg, and 6 oz. of organic sugar and local honey (ratios, to preference); grind the spices and put them in a muslin bag to steep in the wine for 10-12 hrs., straining off several times, intermittently.

Alternatively, cut 8-10 large, aromatic, well-peeled apples into thin slices, put in a tureen; add ¼-½ lb. sugar, 3-4 pepper kernels, the rind of an organic lemon, ⅓ oz. whole cinnamon, 2 oz. peeled and mashed almonds, and four cloves, then pour over 2 750mL bottles of Rhine wine, let it steep with other ingredients until flavor is desirable, filter the wine, serve as a bowl or serve to a party of fine glassware for gathering guests.

HOT BRANDY AND RUM PUNCH

Jerry Thomas, Waldorf-Astoria

For a party of fifteen

1 quart Jamaican rum
1 do. Cognac brandy
1 lb. white loaf-sugar
Juice of 4 lemons
1 tsp. nutmeg

Rub the sugar over the lemons until is has absorbed all the yellow part of the skins, then put the sugar into a punch-bowl; add the ingredients well together, pour the boiling water over the, stir well together; add the rum, brandy and nutmeg; mix thoroughly, and the punch will be ready to serve. As we have said before, it is very important, in making a good punch, that all the ingredients are thoroughly incorporated; and to insure success, the process of mixing must be diligently attended to. Allow a quart for four persons, but this guideline must be taken cum grano salis, for the capacities for persons for this kind of beverage are generally supposed to vary considerably.

Mix the ingredients well together in a large bowl, and you have a splendid punch

HOT BUTTERED PISCO
PDT

6 oz. Hot Water
2 oz. Spiced Pisco 📖
1 tsp. Vanilla Butter 📖

Add everything into a pre-warmed heat-proof mug and stir until the vanilla butter dissolves. Top with sweetened whipped cream. Garnish with finely grated nutmeg.

HOT BUTTERED RUM
Waldorf Astoria

1 Demerara sugar cube
1 lemon peel
2 oz. navy-strength rum
1 dollop unsalted butter *about the size of a sugar cube*
5 whole cloves
5 allspice berries
1 cinnamon stick

Add sugar cube to a ceramic mug and enough boiling water to dissolve. Snap lemon peel, and rub around rim of each cup then drop it in. Add rum and butter, stir to integrate. Add spices, top with boiling water, then stir to mix well (may use a Vitamix). Serve hot. Garnish with freshly-grated nutmeg.

HOT GROG
For each serving:

1 jigger bourbon
2 to 4 cloves
1 cinnamon stick *will also act as a muddler*
1 slice of lemon
½ cup hot water
1 small lump sugar

Into a mug combine bourbon and cloves. Garnish mug with lemon slice and cinnamon stick. Add hot water just before serving.

To flame, lay a teaspoon across cup, put in sugar lump and warm bourbon. Light the sugar cube and gently transfer flaming mixture to the top of the grog.

HOT HOPPELPOPPEL
Schmidt

Heat to the point of boiling, 1 qt. of organic sweetened cream and 3 tablespoons powdered sugar. In a separate bowl, beat into thick foam the yolks of 4 fresh organic eggs with a small splash (½ eggshell) of organic milk. Add a pint of delicious rum. Serve hot in ceramic mugs with a stick of cinnamon and freshly-grated nutmeg.

HOT RUM PUNCH, VARIATION
Waldorf-Astoria

½ portion Oleo Saccharum 📖
8 oz. Jamaican rum
4 oz. VS cognac
2 oz. Combier kümmel
2 oz. Bènèdictine liqueur
48 oz. boiling water

Add oleo saccharum to heat-proof container and dissolve with 1 cup of boiling water. Add the spirits and stir to integrate, adding the remaining hot water. Serve in warmed ceramic mugs. Garnish with fresh citrus slices.

HOT SPICED RUM
Jerry Thomas

1 tsp. sugar
1 wineglass of Jamaican rum
1 tsp. mixed spices *allspice and cloves*
1 piece of butter as large as half of a chestnut.

In a small saucepan, dissolve the sugar in a little water, bring to boil, then remove from heat, add the butter, rum, and spices. Stir until consistent texture, pour off into a heatproof mug, then top with piping hot water, to fill.

KALTSCHALEN, THE CHERRY BISHOP, NO. 479
Schmidt

Remove the pits of 1 ½ quarts of fine sour cherries, break one part of the pits, put the cherries and pits with 1 pint of wine, 1 ½ quarts of water, 6 oz. of sugar, some cinnamon sticks and lemon peel in a tureen; let all boil until the cherries are perfectly soft, then stir a tablespoon of corn starch into cold water, mix that, while continually stirring, to the cherries, let boil a while; strain through a sieve, then put on ice. When serving, add broken Zwieback, cherries steamed in wine, and sugar, snowballs of the beaten whites of eggs, seasoned with lemon sugar, etc.

MISSISSIPPI PUNCH
Waldorf-Astoria

1 ½ oz. Courvoisier VSOP cognac
3/4 Appleton Estate 12 yr. Old rum
3/4 oz. bourbon
1/2 oz. simple syrup

1/2 fresh-squeezed lemon juice

Shake with ice, then strain into an ice-filled Old Fashioned glass. Garnish with an orange wheel and seasonal fruit.

MRS. KITZEL
Parsons

A hot-buttered rum, of sorts.

2 oz. spiced Rum
1 oz. Amaro Nonino
1 tsp. brown sugar
1 thick strip of lemon zest
1 thick strip of orange zest
3 dashes Urban Moonshine maple bitters *-or-* Apple Bitters
Hot local apple cider
1 tbsp. unsalted butter

Combine first 6 ingredients in a charming mug. Whisk until sugar is dissolved. Fill with hot apple cider, add the butter and continue to whisk until it has thoroughly melted and evenly distributed. Garnish with a cinnamon stick and freshly grated nutmeg.

MULLED WINE
WITHOUT EGGS
Jerry Thomas, Waldorf-Astoria, classic

To every pint of water allow:
1 tumblerful of water
Sugar and spice to taste.

In making preparations like the above, it is very difficult to give the exact proportions of ingredients like sugar and spice, as what quantity might best suit one person would be to another quite distasteful.

Boil the spice in the water until the flavor is sufficiently extracted, then add the wine and sugar, and bring the whole to the boiling point, then serve with srips of crsip dry toast or with biscuits.

The spices usual used for mulled wine are cloves, grated nutmeg, allspice, and cinnamon or mace. (*NOTE: or any from the list of Wintry Spices). Any kind of wind may be mulled, but port or claret are those usually selected for the purpose; and the latter [frequently] requires a larger proportion of sugar. The vessel that the wine is boiled in must be diligently clean.

MULLED WINE, A WILDCRAFTER'S TAKE
Han

6 mandarin oranges
2 dried California bay leaves -or- 4 Turkish bay leaves
2 cinnamon sticks
2 tsp. fennel seeds
2 tsp. pink peppercorns, lightly crushed
2/3 cup raw sugar -or- equivalent-to-taste Lamb Sugarworks Dark Robust maple syrup
2 bottles of Pinot Noir

Combine into a large pot with only 1 cup of the wine, simmer over medium heat, stir continuously to dissolve and evenly distribute sugar. Stir in remaining red wine, but do not boil. Fine-strain into heat-proof glass bottles and discard the solids.

NEGUS
Schmidt

1/2 rind of lemon -or- orange
8 oz. sugar
1 pint port wine
1/4 nut of freshly-grated nutmeg

Put the rind into a tureen, add the sugar, port, and nutmeg. Infuse for at least an hour, then add 1 quart of boiling water. Serve immediately in a heat-proof punch bowl (i.e tureen).

NEGUS, ANOTHER
Schmidt

Into a pot, pour 2 bottles of claret, 2 sticks of cinnamon, 6 whole cloves, a pinch of pulverized cardamom (sans pods, using a mortar and pestle), a bit of freshly-grated nutmeg, and a 1/2 pound of organic sugar (which you have already rubbed the rind of a lemon into). Cover, warm over a slow fire (medium heat) to a boil. Once the boil happens, remove from heat, strain, add 1 pint of boiling water, the juice of 1 1/2 lemons, and serve in heat-proof pre-warmed glasses with handles or ceramic mugs.

NEW ORLEANS' MILK PUNCH
PDT, Waldorf-Astoria

1/5 oz. whole milk
1 oz. cognac
1 oz. dark rum
3/4 oz. simple syrup

Shake with ice and strain into a chilled rocks glass filled with one large cube. Garnish with grated nutmeg.

PORT WINE NEGUS
Jerry Thomas

To every pint of port wine allow:
1 quart of boiling water
1/4 lb. of loaf-sugar
1 lemon
Grated nutmeg to taste

Put the wine into a jug, rub some lumps of sugar (equal to 1/4 lb.) on the lemon rind until all the yellow part of the skin is absorbed, then squeeze the juice and strain it. Add the sugar and lemon-juice

MULLED WINE
(IN VERSE)

ADAPTED FROM JERRY THOMAS

First, my dear friend, you must take
Nine eggs, which carefully you'll break —
Into a bowl you'll drop the white,
The yolks into another by it.
Let your companion beat the whites with a switch,
Til they appear quite frothed and rich —
Another's hand the yolks must beat
With sugar, which will make them sweet;
Three or four spoonful may be'll do,
Though some, perhaps, would take but two.
Into a skillet next you'll pour
A bottle of good wine, perhaps more —
Put half a pint of water, too,
Or it may prove to strong, forsooth;
And while the eggs (by two) are beating;
But when it comes to boiling heat,
The yolks and whites together bat
With half a pint of water more
Mixing them well, then gently pour
Into the skillet with the wine,
And stir it briskly all the time.
Then pour it off into a pitcher;
Grate nutmeg to make it all the richer.
Then drink it hot, for he's the fool,
Who lets such precious liquor cool.

to the port wine, with the grated nutmeg; pour over it the boiling water, cover the jug, and when the beverage has cooled a little, it will be fit for use. Negus may also be made of sherry, or any other sweet wine, but it is more usually made of port. This beverage derives its name from Colonel Francis Negus, who is said to have invented it circa 1720s.

ROYAL PUNCH
Jerry Thomas

1 pint hot green tea
½ do. brandy
½ do. Jamaica rum
1 wine-glass of curaçao
1 pint arrack
Juice of 2 limes
A thin slice of lemon
White sugar to taste
¼ pint of warm calf's-foot jelly -or-
    whites of 2 eggs, well beaten

To be drunk as HOT as possible. This is a composition worthy of a king, and the materials are admirably blended; the inebriating effects of the spirits being pacified by the green tea, whilst the jelly softens the mixture and negates to acrimony of the acid and sugar. The whites of a couple of eggs (well beaten to a healthy froth), may be substituted for the jelly where that is not on hand. If the punch is too strong, add more green tea to taste.

RUMFUSTIAN
Jerry Thomas

1 quart strong ale
1 pint gin
1 bottle of sherry
12 eggs
12 large lumps of sugar
1 stick of cinnamon

1 freshly-grated nutmeg
1 lemon

Whisk up the yolks of the eggs until light and frothy, then slowly incorporate first, the gin, then the ale, then gently pour into ceramic mugs. In a saucepan, warm the sherry with the spices, sugar, and lemon peeled very thin stirring continuously and allowing sugar to thoroughly dissolve; after it comes to a boil, pour it into the ceramic mugs and serve a round up to friends with good cheer and much merriment. Drink while hot.

SAPAZEAU PUNCH
Schmidt

Lightly rub the rind of 4 fine organic oranges on ½ lb. loaf sugar; pulverize the relocate to a pot with the juice of the fruits. Add 6 organic eggs and the yolks of 4; beat the mixture well over the heat, adding in 1 ½ qts. of wine of the Rhine, and continue to beat until thickened and frothy. Remove from heat and add 1 cup of maraschino liqueur. Serve Sapazeau hot in heatproof glasses.

SNOWFLAKES PUNCH
Schmidt

Heat 2 750mL bottles of either Moselle -or- Rhine wine wine some lemon peel and 4 oz. organic sugar. In a separate bowl, beat to a thick foam the whites of 4 eggs and ½ teaspoon fresh-squeezed lemon juice. With a spoon, take off small snowballs from the foam and place them in the near-boiling wine, then carefully lift them out with a slotted-spoon after they have soaked up a little wine. In a separate bowl, beat (until uniform consistency) the yolks of the 4 eggs with a tablespoon of the wine, then incorporate with the hot wine, continuously stirring. Pour the warmed wine into a serving bowl, then gently top with the snowballs, then garnish with freshly-grated cinnamon.

SPICED CRANBERRY PUNCH ☆

Natalie Jacob

3 cups of gin or vodka
12 oz. spiced cranberry juice *(see below)*
8 oz. Domaine de Canton ginger liqueur
4 oz. simple syrup
2 oz. freshly-squeezed lemon juice
2 cups of soda water *-or-* sparkling wine *-or-* champagne
cranberries, lemon wheels, and rosemary for garnish

Assemble directly into your punch bowl or large pitcher.

Combine the gin or vodka, cranberry juice, Domaine De Canton Ginger Liqueur, simple syrup and lemon juice into a punch bowl filled with ice.

Use a bundt pan to make a large infused ice cube with rosemary, orange, lemon, and cranberries. This is easy to make in advance and ensures that your punch stays colder longer. Finally, add your club soda. If you want to make this punch a tad bit boozier, you can replace the club soda with champagne or your favorite sparkling wine.

TO MAKE: SPICED CRANBERRY JUICE

4 (12 oz.) bags frozen or fresh cranberries
8 cups of water
10 sprigs of fresh rosemary
1 organic orange
2 cinnamon sticks
2 star anise
½ tsp. whole cloves

To make the cranberry juice, combine the cranberries with 4 cups of water in a large pot. Cook over medium-high heat, stirring frequently so you don't burn the fruit. When the cranberries soften and become mushy, add the remaining 4 cups of water, fruit, herbs, and spices. Bring the mixture to a boil, remove from heat and let completely cool. Strain the juice into a glass bottle, discarding the berries, herbs, and spices. Cover and refrigerate for up to 2 weeks.

POUSSES

A "pousse-cafe" is a digestif in which the liqueurs are layered and provide
a unique drinking experience of multi-colored layers due to the differing
densities of each ingredient. These cocktails require concentrated effort to
prepare properly, and so should be attempted with great care in more intimate
settings, rather than for large parties. Fashion by gently pouring each liquor
over the back of a spoon to avoid mixing layers, beginning with those with
higher specific gravities (higher dissolved sugar and less alcohol) to those with
lower specific gravities (higher alcohol with less sugars). Pousse-cafes predate
the mid-1800s; legend has it that they were invented in New Orleans by
celebrated mixologist, Santina, as a way of visually entertaining his guests.

ANGELS' KISS

Savoy

¼ crème de cacao
¼ brandy
¼ crème de violette
¼ sweet cream

Pour each layer very carefully into an
elegant even-sided glass so that the
ingredients do not mix and they are able
to form 4 distinct delicious layers.

POUSSE L'AMOUR

Jerry Thomas

Fill a small wine-glass half-full with maraschino liqueur, then carefully add the pure
yolk of an egg, surround the egg by gently
pouring over vanilla cordial ensuring
that each liqueur does not stir to the one
beneath it thus creating 3 distinct layers,
then top with Cognac brandy.

Float each layer on top in an elegant
cocktail glass.

SANTA'S NEW ORLEANIAN POUSSE CAFE

Jerry Thomas

⅓ cognac
⅓ Maraschino
⅓ curaçao

Float each layer on top in an elegant
cocktail glass.

CELEBRATED PARISIAN POUSSE CAFE

Jerry Thomas

⅓ curaçao
⅓ Kirschwasser *German Cherry Liqueur*
⅓ Chartreuse

Float each layer on top in an elegant
cocktail glass.

SYLLABUBS

A Sylllabub is a unique ilk of cocktail in which the drink is crafted, in a shared vessel, to partner well with a scrumptious dessert I've included an introduction to them here in hopes that their memory is resurfaced and that you may be inspired to invent your own! (and share with us to be included in future editions). They make a fabulously delicious alternative to traditional dessert-digestif pairings, and if done well, create superb adventures for your guests' taste buds.

THE MERRY SYLLABUB
The Hawk and the Owl

This take on the traditional English after-dinner cocktail is made of hand-whipped organic milk or cream; best wine, cider, or palpably-delicious sherry; sweetened conscientiously; flavoured with seasonal herbs, Christmas spices, artisan-crafted liqueurs, digestifs, or such (i.e. Italian Amaretto); and a right proportion of fresh-squeezed lemon juice. Shaken well until light and frothy and served in a cocktail glass over bite-size house-cookies (i.e. almond macaroons).

A SIMPLE SYLLABUB
Joy, 1964

1 tbsp. sugar syrup
1 ½ oz. top milk
2 oz. heavy cream
½ cup sherry, port, madeira, -or- bourbon
Cookies of choice, frozen for at least one hour prior to serving *optional*

Shake until well-beaten in a bar glass (perhaps over some delicious crumbled cookies, as preferred), serve at once in punch glasses for a party of four.

DRINKING CHOCOLATES, ELIXIRS, AND TEAS

THE BODLEIAN
inspired by Metolius Artisan Tea

assam black tea
cardamom, whole pods
licorice root, dried and cut into 1/4"
   slivers
red pepper, whole
star anise, whole
madagascar vanilla bean

Combine into muslin bag, steep with 12 oz.
hot water in a teapot for 3-5 minutes. Add
warm milk and a spot of sugar (to taste).
Serve hot with scones, clotted cream, and
house-made blackberry jam.

HOT CHOCOLATE
de la Foret

1/4 cup 100% cacao powder
1 tsp. cinnamon powder
2 tbsp. local butter -or- coconut oil
1 tbsp. vanilla extract
1 tbsp. honey, to taste

Put 2 cups of water in a medium saucepan
on high heat. When the water nears
boiling (very hot, but not bubbles are not
breaking the surface), whisk in the cocoa
powder and the cinnamon. Once fully
incorporated, remove from heat and add
in the butter, vanilla extract, and honey.
Stir to combine until the butter has melted
and it and the honey are well-distributed.

Pour into a blender, and loosely adjust top
so that steam can escape, blend on high
for 30 seconds until super-frothy. Pour
into heat-proof ceramic cups. Garnish
with organic marshmallows, if preferred.

MOON OF LONG NIGHTS
The Hawk and the Owl

6 oz. milk, warmed, piping hot but
   not burnt
1- 1 1/2 " vanilla beans, split lengthwise
1 tsp. dried lavender
2 oz. protein
2 oz. fats

In a cast iron skillet, warm up the milk,
continuously stirring so as not to scald,
add the other ingredients once the milk
becomes warm. Sip as you prepare for a
long winter's sleep.

For: lavender, sleeping, rest, rejuvenation,
long nights; experience the darkness and
its renewal in preparation of the coming of
the light and the expectation of miracles.

OXFORDSHIRE TEA
The Hawk and the Owl

2 tsp. Assam black tea
1 oz. essence of bergamot

Combine into muslin bag, steep with 16
oz. hot water in a teapot for 3-5 minutes.
Add warm milk and a spot of sugar,
serve hot with scones, clotted cream, and
house-made raspberry jam and half a
chilled orange, sliced.

SACRED HOT CHOCOLATE
The Hawk and the Owl

inspired by DIY Bitters

powdered cacao
8-10 oz. piping hot water *-or-* milk, warmed
1 tsp. local honey
1 tbsp. **Cacao Bitters** 🍫
Measure to preference and sweeten to taste.

WARMED GOLDEN MILK
de la Foret

2 tbsp. ghee *-or-* ¼ cup coconut milk
1 tsp. turmeric powder
½ tsp. ginger powder
Pinch of freshly ground black pepper, finely with mortar and pestle
2 cups milk *nix if using coconut milk*
pinch of freshly-ground cardamom
1 tsp. cinnamon to taste *korintje, saigon, vietnamese, or ceylon*

Melt the ghee in a small saucepan over medium-high heat. Add the spices and stir continuously for 30 seconds or until fragrant. Add the milk, stir constantly (especially scraping the bottom of the pan) until piping hot. Remove from heat and stir in honey until fully dissolved. Place in a blender, with top slightly ajar to release steam, for about 30 seconds until frothy and uniformly golden. Pour into heat-proof ceramic cups and enjoy immediately.

WENDELL BERRY, FOR TWO
(AKA "SLEEPYTIME")

inspired by Celestial Seasonings

1 tsp. chamomile
1 tsp. spearmint
1 tsp. lemongrass
1 tsp. Tilia flowers
1 tsp. blackberry leaves
1 tsp. orange blossoms
1 tsp. hawthorn
1 tsp. rosehips

Combine into muslin bag, steep with 16 oz. hot water in a teapot for 5-6 minutes. Serve hot with scones, clotted cream, and house-made marionberry jam.

WOLF MOON
The Hawk and the Owl

4 oz. house-made chicken stock with added vegetables
½ oz. fresh-squeezed lemon juice
Pinch of cayenne
Bouquet Garni

Warm in a pot, then pour into a ceramic mug. Serve piping hot. Drink whilst hot.

FROM THE
KING OF POPS BAR

FRESH FOR THE SEASON

"The King of Pops bar is located in the marvelous historic building of Ponce City Market in the center of Atlanta along the BeltLine within Old 4th Ward. We are in the process of opening additional locations at cool spots throughout the South. At our bars, we craft simple seasonal recipes into which we can 'drop a pop' to create our beloved 'poptails.' Come visit us!"

-Mitchell Oliver
"BOJANGLES" THE TREE ELF
KING OF POPS BAR MANAGER, PONCE CITY MARKET

SLUSHIES

Simply mix the ingredients listed with a handful of ice and throw it in the blender for about 30-45 seconds. If you really want to get fancy, get yourself a slushie machine. "Trust me," Mitchell says, "the investment will pay dividends as you become everyone's favorite party host!"

HO HO, JOE
Mitchell Oliver

4 parts cold brew
1 part Kahlua
1 part B-scott Schnapps
3/4 parts Amaretto

SANTA'S CIDER
Mitchell Oliver

4 parts apple cider
1 part Jack Fire
1 part bourbon,
1/8 part lemon

PUMP-KING SPICE LATTE
Mitchell Oliver

milk
pumpkin puree
Kahlua
vodka
pumpkin pie spice
cinnamon

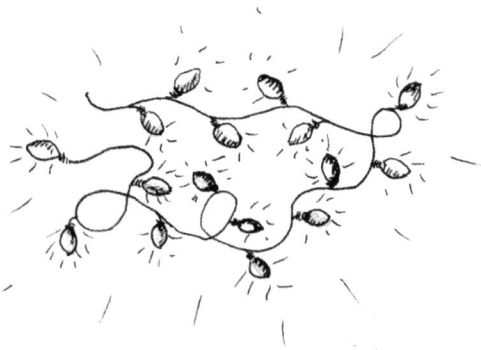

POPTAILS

Into an empty glass, drop the pop and add a light amount of ice. Then, in a mixing glass, add ingredients and shake 10-15 seconds, strain over ice and pop, and Enjoy!

KENTUCKY NOG
Mitchell Oliver

4 parts eggnog
2 parts bourbon
Dash of cinnamon
Splash of salted brown syrup
w/ vanilla/ eggnog pop

CRAN-ORANGE MARG (AKA THE ELF-A-RITA)
Mitchell Oliver

1 tequila
½ triple
1 orange
2 cran
¼ lime
w/ fruit pop

JAM SESSION
NY Brewing Co. bartender

1 ½ oz. gin
½ oz. elderflower
Concord grape
lemon
soda
w/ blueberry lemon pop

DASHING PUMPKINS
Mitchell Oliver

Vanilla-infused Vodka (see pg. ...)
Kahlua
Cream
Pumpkin puree
Pumpkin pie spice
w/ pumpkin chai latte pop

AMARILLO BY MORNING
Mitchell Oliver

2 oz. xx tequila
2 oz. apple cider
½ oz. fresh-squeezed lemon juice
½ oz. maple syrup
cinnamon
w/ caramel apple pop

ITALIAN RACE CAR
Mitchell Oliver

(sweeeeet)

1 ½ oz. Amaretto
1 ½ oz..Kahlua
1 oz. milk
 float Banjo Cold Brew

LUCHA LECHE
Mitchell Oliver

4 oz. horchata
2 oz. spiced rum
½ oz. salted brown syrup
w/ a vanilla pop

HONEY CRISP
Mitchell Oliver

2 oz. apple brandy *Calvados*
2 oz. apple cider
½ oz. fresh-squeezed lemon juice
½ oz. pure maple syrup
w/ a fruity pop

BACKBAR

BB

BACKBAR

As follows are a few "backbar" items that are called for in the above concoctions, and also with which you may create and build your own winter libations!

I highly recommend the use of organics, fair-trade, and hyper-local products in the creation of artisan cocktails. Such intentionality around selecting ingredients really impacts the quality of the final product. Please remember, especially during this Christmas season, that everything is sourced from somewhere and someone. All such choices affect your relationship to the earth and other people's work. Be mindful of your relationships to your supply chain. It is better to source well and craft fewer cocktails, then otherwise. Such is my belief. For some reason "doing the right thing" also tastes much better!

LIQUORS AND LIQUEURS

APPLE, PEAR, AND ORANGE PEEL-INFUSED BOURBON

2 Fuji apples
1 Bosc pear *ripened appropriately*
1 whole orange rind *peeled, with as little pith as possible*
1 750mL bottle of bourbon

Wash fruit; core and chop apples and pear. Place in airtight glass container along with the orange peel. Add bourbon. Allow to sit for at least 10 days, stirring occasionally. Fine-strain and funnel back into bottle.

CELTIC NOCINO

2 lbs. unripe walnuts, quartered
1 cup Meyer lemon zest strips
½ cup chopped spruce tips
3 tbsp. crushed dried spice-brush berries
1 ½ tsp. chopped sassafras root
2-3 quarts high-proof vodka

Best to start on the Summer Solstice, so that this concoction is ready by the Winter Solstice. Stir all the ingredients into a 1-gallon glass jar. Let steep for 40 days in a cool, dark place.

Strain out and discard the solids. Measure the liquid and combine with an about-equal amount of simple syrup. Let steep for 3 months. Fine-strain into storage bottles. The flavor will improve over 6 months.

CHRISTMAS TREE SPIRIT WINTER GIN
Han

2 tbsp. juniper berries
1 750mL bottle of vodka
2 tsp. coriander seeds
1 tsp. orange peel *dried, cut, and sifted*
3 inch sprig fresh white fir *-or-* pine *-or-* spruce *whichever is locally available*

1 cinnamon stick
1 whole allspice berry
1 dried sage leaf
1 dried bay leaf

Place the juniper berries in a 1L (qt.)
glass jar, pour vodka over them and
cap tightly. Allow to sit for 12 hours; add
the remaining ingredients and let sit for
another 36 hours. Fine-strain, bottle, and
store in cool dry place for up to 1 year.

CINNAMON VODKA

Place 1 750mL bottle of unflavored vodka
and 2 cinnamon sticks in an airtight
wide-mouth non-reactive glass container;
stir every other day for a week. Strain,
and funnel vodka back into the original
vodka bottle. Lasts indefinitely (except
"not really," because it's such a delicious
augmentation to the Christmas season).

COFFEE-BEAN
INFUSED VODKA

Add 1 cup espresso beans and 1 cup
French roast coffee beans to airtight
glass jar. Add 32 oz. unflavored vodka
and infuse for no more than 7 days. Fine-
strain and funnel back into bottle. Date.
Will last 6 months or so.

DOUGLAS FIR LIQUEUR
Han

2 large handfuls conifer tips -or- needles, roughly chopped (pine, spruce, fir,
  Douglas fir)
½ cup dried hawthorn berries -or- 1
  cup fresh
2 whole allspice berries
1 750mL bottle vodka
1 cup simple syrup

Combine dry ingredients into a clean 1L
glass jar, pour vodka into the jar,

sure all ingredients are completely
submerged. Cap the jar tightly and store
in a cool, dry place for 1-2 weeks, shaking
daily. Fine-strain, then stir in simple syrup.
Age for at least 1 week, then bottle (date)
and store for up to 1 year.

FIG AND VANILLA RUM
Han

1 pound fresh Black Mission figs
½ vanilla bean, split lengthwise
1 750mL bottle of aged gold rum

Combine the figs and vanilla in a clean 1L
(quart) glass jar. Pour the rum into the jar,
insuring the figs are wholly submerged
and there are no air pockets. Cap the jar
tightly and store in a cool, dry place for at
least 1 month, shaking daily and making
sure figs continue to be submerged.
Fine-strain (the discarded figs may make
a tasty topping for vanilla ice cream), then
bottle (date) and store for up to 1 year.

GINGER AND
LEMONGRASS-
INFUSED BAINBRIDGE
DISTILLERY GIN
orig. G'Vine Floraison

½ cup peeled and chopped fresh
  ginger
12 lemongrass leaves cleaned and
  chopped into thirds
1 750mL bottle Bainbridge
  Distillery Gin

Add all ingredients into a large, airtight,
glass container. Seal, stir occasionally,
store for 10 days. Double-strain, then
funnel back into bottle. Date. Will keep
fresh for up to 2 months.

GINGERBREAD BOURBON
The Hawk and the Owl

1 750mL bottle of bourbon
¼ cup dark molasses
¼ teaspoon cloves
½ teaspoon cinnamon
½ teaspoon freshly-grated nutmeg
1 teaspoon ginger powder

First, pour off about 6-8 oz of bourbon by using in another recipe or enjoying on the rocks!

Then, add warmed molasses and spices to bottle, recork, shake vigorously to incorporate and dissolve. Label bottle of bourbon anew, "Gingerbread Bourbon," and set to use!

MNEMOSYNE'S ROSEMARY WINE
Han

3 sprigs fresh and tender rosemary
3 ¼ cups enjoyable dry white wine

Rinse the rosemary thoroughly, pat dry to remove moisture. Gently open the rosemary by pressing on the leaves with a rolling pin to release their flavor and aroma. Decant 1 goblet of wine from the bottle, then slip the sprigs into the bottle, funnel as much wine back in to cover the sprigs. Re-cork the bottle and store in a cool, dark place for 1-2 weeks, checking to insure rosemary is under the wine line. Fine-strain. Makes a pleasant little aperitif!

PEACH AND PECAN BOURBON
Han

3 medium Georgia peaches
2 tbsp. brown sugar
750mL bottle good-quality bourbon

HISTORY

MEASURE THIS!

(BARTENDING MEASUREMENTS THROUGH THE AGES)

1 DASH = ⅙ TEASPOON
1 BAR SPOON = 1 TEASPOON
1 PONY = 1 OZ.
1 JIGGER = 1 ½ OZ
1 BAR GLASS = 1 ½ OZ

1 cup raw shelled Georgia pecans

Wash, peel, and chop peaches, scrape out and discard the pits (insure no wayward pieces of pit remain!). Combine peaches, sugar, and bourbon in a clean 1L (quart) glass jar. Store in a cool, dry place for 1 week, shaking it daily and making sure the peaches stay submerged in the bourbon. After 1 week has passed, prepare pecans. Soak pecans in a bowl for 30 minutes (this will help remove the bitterness). Preheat oven to 350°F, with rack in the middle. Strain pecans and pat them dry. Spread pecans in an even layer on a baking sheet. Toast in the oven about 10 minutes, stirring with a wooden spoon every few minutes until aromatic and golden brown. Allow to cool then finely chop with a knife or in a food processor. Add pecans to the jar of peaches and bourbon. Store in a cool, dark place for 3 to 7 days, shaking it daily to insure all ingredients submerged in alcohol. Fine-strain, bottle (date), and store in a cool, dark place for up to 1 year.

SPICED PERUVIAN PISCO
1 750mL bottle Pisco
1 3-inch orange peel
1 split vanilla bean
1 tsp. black peppercorns
1 tsp. cloves
1 tsp. allspice berries
1 tsp. star anise kernels
1 cinnamon stick

Combine in a non-reactive container and infuse, covered for 24 hours at room temperature. Fine-strain and bottle.

SPRUCE TIP VODKA
1 cup feathery young spruce tips
1 750mL bottle of vodka

Place spruce tips into blender and add just enough vodka to cover them. Blend until

pulverized, then pour the green liquid into a glass jar and top off with the remaining vodka. Shake to distribute, then allow to steep in cool dark corner for about 2-4 days. Fine-strain off the vodka, and discard the spruce tips.

VANILLA BEAN-INFUSED ORIGINAL DARK RUM

Split one bean lengthwise, being mindful of not wasting seeds. Gently scrape out the seeds with the point of the knife, and place beans and seeds into a bottle of dark rum. Agitate every day or two for 7 days, then it's ready for use!

VANILLA BEAN-INFUSED VODKA

Split one bean lengthwise, being mindful of not wasting seeds. Gently scrape out the seeds with the point of the knife, and place beans and seeds into a bottle of your favorite unflavored vodka. Agitate every day or two for 7 days, then it's ready for use!

VERMOUTH, A WILDCRAFTERS' TAKE (DRY)

Han

Peel of 1 medium lemon *cut in wide strips*
Peel of 1/4 southern grapefruit *cut in wide strips*
Wormwood -or 1 tbsp. finely chopped fresh tarragon
1 tbsp. dried lemon balm
1 tbsp. dried elderberries
1 tbsp. dried hyssop
1 tbsp. dried rose petals
1 tsp. dried chamomile flowers
1 tsp. dried lavender flowers
1 750mL bottle of quality dry white wine, divided
1/4 cup simple syrup
250mL *(1 cup + 1 tbsp.)* of Cognac

Combine the lemon peel, grapefruit peel, wormwood/tarragon, lemon balm, elderberries, hyssop, rose petals, chamomile and lavender flowers, and 1 cup of the wine into a medium saucepan. Bring to a boil over medium heat, then reduce to low and simmer for 5 minutes. Remove from heat, then let thoroughly cool. Fine-strain, then combine with the remaining white wine into a clean saucepan. Bring to a boil (again) over medium heat and gradually stir in the simple syrup with a wooden spoon. Remove from heat and stir in the Cognac. Let cool completely, then bottle and store in the refrigerator for up to 2 months. Age at least 1 full day before enjoying. May be enjoyed simply in a small ice-filled glass or with a splash of soda and a twist of lemon. Or any of the other recipes found in this cocktail book calling for Dry Vermouth (i.e. a martini).

VERMOUTH, A WILDCRAFTERS' TAKE (SWEET)

Han

1/2 cup dried Black Mission figs, chopped
1 vanilla bean *split lengthwise, and cut into 1" pieces*
1 cup Armagnac
Peel of 1 medium orange *cut into wide strips*
1/2 tsp. dried bee balm *-or-* 1/4 tsp. dried mint -or 1/4 tsp. dried oregano
1/2 tsp. dried mugwort
1 tsp. dried sage
1 cinnamon stick
1 whole clove
2 whole star anise pods
1/2 dried California bay leaf *-or-* 1 Turkish bay leaf *torn into pieces*
1 750mL bottle of delectable dry white wine, divided
1/4 cup caramelized simple syrup, more as needed

Combine the figs, vanilla beans, and Armagnac in a clean glass container. Cover tightly and store for 2 days in a cool, dark place. Fine strain the mixture, then set aside in a covered jar. Combine the orange peel, bee balm, mugwort, sage, cinnamon, clove, star anise, bay leaf, and 1 cup of the wine into a medium saucepan. Bring to a boil over medium heat, then reduce to low and simmer for 5 minutes. Remove from heat, then let thoroughly cool. Fine-strain, then combine with the remaining white white in a clean saucepan. Bring to a boil (again) over medium heat and gradually stir in the carmelized simple syrup with a wooden spoon. Remove from heat and stir in the Armagnac Let cool completely, sweeten further if desired, then bottle and store in the refrigerator for up to 2 months. Age at least 1 full day before enjoying. May be enjoyed in any of the other recipes found in this cocktail book calling for Sweet Vermouth (i.e. a manhattan).

VIN DE NOIX
Han

6-8 green walnuts *available in May, June, -or- July depending on local climate*
Peel of 1/4 medium orange, cut into wide strips
1 inch piece of vanilla bean
1 small whole cloves
A ½ stick of cinnamon
½ cup sugar, *-or- more, to taste*
½ cup *(120mL)* **of vodka**
1 750mL bottles of dry red wine
(use a cutting board that you don't mind staining yellow, and handle with care everything green walnuts may touch)

Rinse and dry the walnuts. Carefully cut them in half using a large sturdy knife or Chinese cleaver. Split the vanilla bean open (be mindful to conserve the tiny precious seeds). Combine the walnuts, orange peel, vanilla, clove, cinnamon, and sugar in a clean 1L (quart) glass container. Pour the vodka and wine into the jar, making sure the walnuts are wholly submerged and there are no air pockets. Cap the jar tightly and store in a cool, dark place for 1 month, shaking it daily and making sure walnuts continue to be submerged. Fine-strain, sweeten if desired, then bottle (date) and store for up to 1 year. Age for at least 3 months before serving, and will improve with age. Serve in small delicate glasses, chilled or at room temperature.

VIN D'ORANGE
Han

2 large navel oranges *preferably Cara*

Cara
1 small regional grapefruit
½ vanilla bean
½ cup *(100g)* **sugar**
½ cup *(102mL)* **vodka**
¼ cup *(60mL)* **brandy**
1 750mL bottle of nice dry wine *-or- pleasant dry rose*

Rinse and dry the citrus fruits; trim and discard their stem ends. Cut each orange into ¼" thick rounds. Cut the grapefruit in half, then cut each half into ¼" half-circles. Split the vanilla bean, be mindful of the seeds — you want those! Combine the oranges, grapefruit, vanilla, and sugar in a sterilized 1L (quart) glass container. Pour the vodka, brandy, and wine into the jar, push the fruit down with a wooden spoon making sure to wholly submerge it and there are no air pockets. Cap the jar tightly and store in a cool, dark place for 1 month, shaking it daily to moisten the pieces insisting on floating up. Fine-strain, then bottle (date) and store for in the refrigerator for up to 6 months. Age for at least 1 month before imbibing, and will improve with age. Serve chilled, over glassy ice cubes.

WALNUT-INFUSED V.S.O.P. COGNAC
1 750mL V.S.O.P. Cognac
4 oz. raw walnuts

Toast walnuts in small saucepan at approx. 175, turning every 30 seconds. Walnuts are toasted when edges turn brown and black; process will take about 9-10 minutes. Allow walnuts to cool. Combine walnuts with cognac in a large, non-reactive container, then stir, cover, and infuse at room temperature for 48 hours. Fine-strain and bottle.

SHRUBS, ELIXIRS, SYRUPS, & BITTERS

APPLE-CARDAMOM SHRUB
Dietsch

3 apples, peeled and halved
1 cup apple cider vinegar
1/2 cup turbinado sugar
1 tablespoon cardamom seeds, crushed

Shred the apples using a box grater. Add together all ingredients into a non-reactive (glass) container. Leave on countertop for up to 2 days. Fine-strain into clean mason jars. Shake well, then refrigerate. Will keep for 1 year.

BLACK CURRANT SHRUB
Dietsch

1 1/2 cups black currant
3/4 cup raw cane sugar
3/4 cup red wine vinegar

Crush black currants into a bowl with the sugar, stir to incorporate. Then, let sit in the refrigerator for 24hrs. Strain into handled measuring glass with vinegar and whisk well to thoroughly dissolve sugar. Strain out the solids into a clean mason jar. Shake, then place in refrigerator for a week before serving.

BLOOD ORANGE SYRUP
Parsons

1-2 cups raw sugar, to preference
1 cup water
2 blood oranges

Zest and juice the oranges into a medium saucepan, add water and sugar and bring all ingredients to a boil, stirring constantly to keep sugar from burning (although, some caramelization is alright). Remove from heat at first sign of a boil, stirring constantly until cooled to insure that sugar is fully dissolved. Once cool, (you cool?) strain into a glass jar. Store in the refrigerator. Will keep about 3 days, but likely enjoyed upon making!

CACAO BITTERS
2 1/2 oz. cacao tincture
2 oz. hawthorn tincture
2 oz. damiana tincture
1 oz. raw local honey
2 tsp. cinnamon tincture
1/2 tsp. vanilla bean tincture
10 drops gingerroot tincture
10 drops cayenne tincture

CAROB SYRUP
1/2 cup carob powder
2 tablespoons agave nectar
1/2 teaspoon vanilla extract
1 cup water

In a medium saucepan, over medium heat, stir powder into water, constantly stirring while adding agave, until mixture becomes a smooth syrup. Once warmed to a boil. Remove from heat and whisk vivaciously until foamy, add vanilla until well incorporated. Store in a glass jar in the refrigerator for several weeks.

CLOVE SYRUP
Zachos

24 oz. simple syrup

1 ½ oz. whole cloves

In a medium-sized pot, bring simple syrup to a rolling boil, then add cloves and remove from heat. Infuse for 15 minutes, fine-strain, cool, bottle, and store in the refrigerator.

CRANBERRY SAUCE SHRUB
Dietsch

1 large orange
½ cup raw sugar
2 cups (8 oz.) cranberries
1 cup apple cider vinegar
1 cinnamon stick
1 whole nutmeg zested with microplane
½ teaspoon allspice berries cracked
½ tablespoon roughly chopped ginger

Into a bowl, with a peeler add the zest of orange in long strips and the sugar. Muddle together to create an oleo-saccharum. Juice the orange and set aside as you puree the cranberries and vinegar in a blender. Add together all the various ingredients into a non-reactive glass container and place on countertop for 2 days to marinate, shaking periodically to help spices distribute well. Strain off solids, then store in refrigerator until use.

CRANBERRY SIMPLE SYRUP & MACERATED CRANBERRIES

16 oz. simple syrup
1 8 oz. bag of cranberries frozen is fine

Heat the simple syrup until it almost boils, then turn down the heat to medium and add the cranberries. Once the skin of the first few cranberries splits, remove from heat and allow to cool. Bottle a portion of the syrup and reserve the rest to store with the cranberries in the refrigerator.

ELDERBERRY ELIXIR
Han

3 cups fresh elderberries or 1 ½ cups, if dried
¼ cups dried, cut, and sifted rose hips or ½ cup, if fresh
Peel of 2 medium oranges cut in wide strips
2 whole cloves
⅔ cups local honey
2 cups brandy or more, if needed
1 cinnamon stick

Combine all (save brandy and cinnamon) into a sterilized 1L glass jar and stir until honey is well-incorporated. Gradually add the brandy to coat all ingredients and replace any pockets of air. Insure all ingredients are covered by brandy, add more if necessary. Press the cinnamon

THE HOLLY AND THE IVY, VERSE 1

"The holly and the ivy,
When they are both full grown,
Of all the trees that are in the wood,
The holly bears the crown:

The rising of the sun
And the running of the deer,
The playing of the merry organ,
Sweet singing in the choir."

- -TRADITIONAL BRITISH FOLK CHRISTMAS CAROL

HOUSE-MADE GRENADINE

AS EXPLAINED BY THE AUTHOR, EXCITEDLY

INGREDIENTS

At least a dozen pomegranates
Approx. 1 lemon for every 12 pomegranates
Approx. ½ cup sugar for every 12 pomegranates

1. put on some stain-worthy clothes

2. remove all things from area that you don't want accidentally splattered by pome-granate juice, because it travels with wondrous trajectory

3. cover surfaces with newspaper

4. carefully seed the pomegranates into a deep bowl, after 1-2 pomegranates, decant those into a larger {containing} bowl

5. put into a pot, be sure there is at least a 2-3" room above seeds

6. add about 5 cups of water (*or was it 2/ 2 1/2 cups....hmmm....*) basically like a 1:5 cup ratio of water to pomegranate seeds (I think). really, bottom line: just need enough water to cover the bottom 1-2" of the pot so that when you turn up the heat the pomegranate seeds have a viscous base to work with.

7. warm gently on medium heat until it feels like a good warm hot bath for the hands. ie. not too hot but very warm, because...

8. move the seeds around with your hands (*oh yeah, wash your hands and under your nails really really REALLY thoroughly*), if you'd prefer to skip this step (step 8: massage the seeds with your hands until you get all the juice out you can by squeezing them), then just use a wooden spatula and move them around. until warm and thoroughly moved about.

9. turn off the heat

10. immersible blender. BE SURE TO FULLY FEEL THE BLENDER ON THE BOTTOM OF THE POT BEFORE TURNING ON!!! (*or the juice will fling everywhere!*) blend in 3 long batches, foam will form on the of the pot; blend until the entire visible surface area is covered in foam. let the blender cool (on cool surface away from stove) and skim off foam

11. repeat about 3 times until you feel like you've released every morsel of juice from the seed, by the end of this process the seeds will be like fine sand.

12. strain. (*a process within The Process*)

   a. strain using funnel sieve, get the big chunky parts out

   b. strain using a mesh strainer atop funnel sieve, ACTUALLY USE BOTH the 2 metal sieves: small stacked atop medium over the funnel .

   c. repeat this process 3 times. note: this entire process takes several hours so as to thoroughly strain and not waste precious elixir. this is a good time to get other chores done, meals cooked, enjoy dinner (... *all that being said, be sure it is safely protected as not to be bumped over and cause a mess when not in attendance.*)

13. once super-thoroughly strained,

14. put back in pot, onto stove, bring to medium high heat. add like 1-2 cups sugar (*again to some ratio that kinda tastes right, definitely err on less-sweet side, because cocktails can always use added simple syrup, but taking out sweetness is, well, "impossible"*), also

15. fresh squeeze lemon to taste/ balance (*I'd add about 1 lemon for every 1-2 cups sugar. this is a preference thing, again, but, again, i'd err on side of less, just enough for "preservation extension", because citrus can always be made in-the-moment during cocktail prep actualle*).

16. stir until dissolved and balanced; taste frequently at this stage to insure a pleasant (*warm and cozy taste*); have lots of clean spoons on hand for this part of the process.

16. cool.

17. funnel into clean glass bottles -or- bourbon/ gin bottles (in which case the remaining liquor imparts a delightful vibe to the elixir.)

18. ENJOY! (*and refrigerate, up to 1 month, that which is not enjoyed post-haste.*)

19. be sure to share the joy with others and toast the merriment in our hearts.

stick down through the middle of the concoction. Thoroughly wipe clean the rim, then cap the jar tightly and store in a cool, dark place for 1-2 months, shaking occasionally, and insure all ingredients remain submerged in brandy. Fine-strain into a clean glass bottle, date, and may store up to one year. Serve 1oz. "neat" in a brandy glass -or- warm to enjoy as a hot toddy.

Note: ½ teaspoon every few hours may shorten or stave off cold or flu; this recipe yields 2 cups.

EVERGREEN OXYMEL
Han

2 large handfuls conifer needles
harvested in the spring (pine, spruce, fir, Douglas fir; individual trees differ in taste)
1 cup apple cider vinegar
¾ cup local honey, to taste

Roughly cut the conifer needles using kitchen scissors or a good knife. Combine the needles and the vinegar into a sterilized pint glass ball jar, leave ½ headspace, stir with a barspoon to allow vinegar to fill all air pockets and insure all needles are completely submerged.

Wipe the rim extraordinarily clean. Cover the jar with a non-reactive lid and store in a cool dark place for 2-4 weeks. Shaking daily and checking that ingredients remain submerged.

Fine-strain into glass jar with non-reactive lid. May store in refrigerator for up to 1 year.

FIG-CINNAMON SHRUB
Dietsch

1 pint purple figs
1 cup apple cider vinegar

1-2 sticks cinnamon
1 cup raw sugar

Combine all ingredients, excepting sugar, into non-reactive container and allow to sit on countertop for 2 days, shaking periodically. Taste and add more spice, to preference. Strain off solids, add sugar, shake until thoroughly dissolved, store in a sealed glass jar. Allow to sit a week before using. Store in refrigerator.

GINGER SHRUB
Dietsch

½ cup freshly-juiced ginger juice
½ cup apple cider vinegar
⅓ cup raw sugar

Combine in glass jar, shake until sugar is dissolved, ready for use immediately. Enjoy! (to your health!!)

GINGER SYRUP
The Hawk and the Owl

In a medium saucepan, combine 1 cup of water, 1 cup organic fair-trade sugar, and several knobs of freshly-grated ginger, to taste. Bring to a boil, then simmer, stirring often to dissolve sugar. At first crack of a boil, remove from heat. Once cooled, strain into a glass jar, and refrigerate until use.

HONEY SYRUP
1 cup honey
1 cup boiling hot water

Combine the honey and hot water in a bowl and whisk to dissolve. Cool completely then store syrup in a glass jar in the refrigerator for up to 1 month.

ICED HOT CHOCOLATE
The Hawk and the Owl

In a small pot, heat ¾ - ⅓ cup milk (of preferred variety) over medium heat until steaming, stirring constantly and scraping the bottom of the pot with the spatula to avoid scalding. Mix in 3 tablespoons (to preference) sipping chocolate and sweetness (to preference), whisk well until completely melted, incorporated, and mixture is frothy. Allow to cool to room-temperature. Just before serving, ice to chill. Stir vigorously to maintain adequate consistency when making a cocktail with "iced hot chocolate." Should yield about ½ cup to use.

LEMON-LIME SHRUB
Dietsch

1 cup fresh-squeezed lemon juice
  5-6 lemons
¾ cup raw sugar
½ cup fresh-squeezed lime juice
¾ cup champagne vinegar

Zest lemons with peeler into long strips. Place into bowl containing sugar. Muddle together to create an oleo-saccharum. Into a separate bowl, juice the lemons and lime, set aside. Add vinegar and combine, shaking well to blend all ingredients, strain, then add to a glass bottle. Allow 2-3 days for flavors to develop.

NOUGAT SYRUP

2 cups sugar
½ cup light corn syrup
1 cup local honey
1/4 tsp salt
1/4 cup water
2 egg whites *room temperature, to yield ½ cup*
2 tsp vanilla extract
1 tsp almond extract
1 tsp orange blossom water *-or-* rose water
2 tablespoons butter *softened at room temperature*
½ cup whole hazelnuts, toasted
1 cup whole almonds, toasted
½ cup whole pistachios, toasted

Make on a dry day, an electric mixer is nearly imperative. First cook in a 2 qt. saucepan, 2 tablespoons of the sugar, 1 tablespoon water and ½ cup light corn syrup. Blend until boiling. Cover and cook for a few minutes, then over medium heat until forms a soft-ball (about 238 degrees), then let stand while you beat the egg whites until stiff. Then, add syrup gradually to egg whites and continue to beat for 5 minutes. In a separate pan, over low heat, combine 1 cup local honey and 1 cup sugar, bring mixture to about 285, then combine the two mixtures. Add in the extracts and orange blossom/ rose water, salt, beat in the butter, then fold in the nuts. Pour into a buttered pan, dusted with confectioners' sugar; let sit for 12 hours, then cut into preferred sizes. To use as syrup, use before allowing to "set."

OLEO SACCHARUM
4 lemons
1 lime
1 orange
1 southern grapefruit *half, if large*

1 cup sugar

Add all ingredients to non-reactive bowl and muddle well, incorporate sugar (until dissolved), and then rinds. Cover and let sit for at least 2 hours (preferably overnight).

ROSEMARY SYRUP
1 cup sugar
1 cup water
½ cup finely-chopped rosemary

In a medium saucepan, bring the ingredients to a simmer, stirring occasionally to thoroughly dissolve the sugar. At the first crack of a boil, remove from heat and allow to cool completely before straining into a glass jar. May store in refrigerator for up to 1 month.

SORGHUM SIMPLE SYRUP
Parsons

In a medium saucepan, warm 1 part sorghum to 1 part water (to preference), stirring frequently to dissolve, to create a sorghum mix that can substitute for other sweetnesses.

SPRUCE TIP SYRUP
1 cup roughly chopped spruce tips
1 cup water
1 cup sugar

Combine into a saucepan and bring to a gentle boil, then simmer. Whisk to thoroughly dissolve sugar. Remove from heat and allow to cool overnight. Strain and seal into a glass jar.

FROM "IN THE FOREST OF THE FRASER FIRS"

BY ANDRÉ DUBIGNON FURIN

1. There's Magic here
it crossed my mind
that You are not
too far away.

2. I walk among
the Fraser Firs
the taste of snow
fresh off their boughs.

3. Mother Mary Dear
good fortunes find
this forest route
where Frasers sway.

4. The world is young
with monk's glad chorus
our hearts aglow,
{bells and chimes}
"It's Christmas NOW!"
{Emmanuel. Emmanuel!}

———◇———

5. This air I breathe
is fresh and pure
the fragrance sweet
with thoughts of You.

6. On ground I kneel
to offer thanks
to the Lord on High
in this Forest grand,

7. {gentle bells and soft chimes}
"The child conceived.
God's Love endures.

The Prince of Peace.
The Word! Amen!"
{delicate chorus: Glory Alleluia
Glory Glory Emanuel}

8. The Firs conceal
my warm tears wet
that drop beside
me -- in this Forest grand.

———◇———

9. The bells they chime:
The river flows:
I stand up proud:
Like the Fraser Firs,

10. and find the path
that leads the way
back to the tow'rs that ring
from the Abbey's church.

11. [Blessed be]
These Holy times
when on Christmas it snows
In the sacred shroud
of the Fraser Firs.

12. Beyond stained-glass
on Christmas Day
the Forests sing,
too, for our Savior's Birth!
{pipe organ goes wild
and trumpets sound}

WHIPS AND OTHER GARNISHES

HOUSE-MADE MARASCHINO CHERRIES
Stewart

Clean and pit fresh [sour] cherries. Loosely fill a sterilized Mason jar with the cherries. Pour maraschino liqueur (-or- brandy -or- bourbon) over the cherries until they are completely covered. Seal the jar, refrigerate, use within 4 weeks.

VANILLA BUTTER
1 lb. brown sugar
1 lb. unsalted butter
1 qt. vanilla ice cream
2 star anise pods
5 cloves
5 whole allspice berries
5 black peppercorns

Add spices to a pot. Add butter and heat until it melts, then add brown sugar until lumps are gone. Add ice cream and stir until smooth and thick. Strain spices and store in a non-reactive container in the freezer.

WHIPPED CREAM
(SWEETENED)
3 oz. heavy cream
¼ oz. simple syrup

Whip until runny, but not stiff.

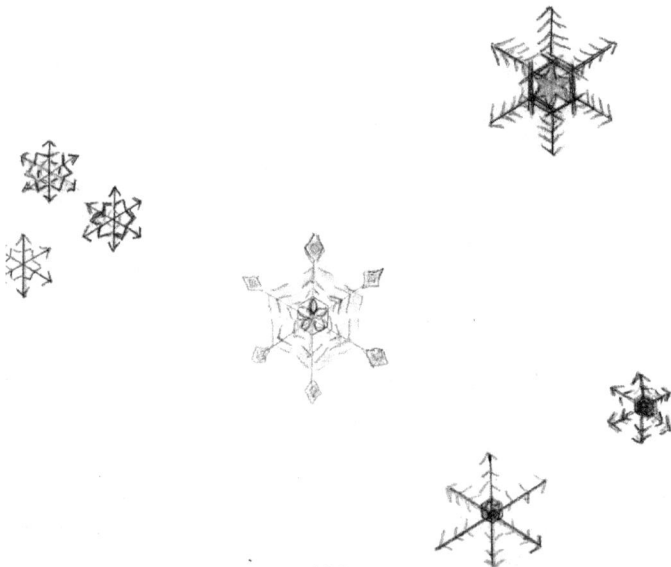

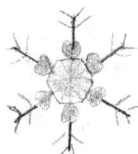

RECIPES

A TASTE OF THE SEASON

Below you will discover a handful of additional non-beverage recipes to accompany your holiday festivities. Most of them are traditional Christmas desserts that have been passed around between friends and among family for many generations. Some of these are recorded on 3x5 index cards or odd scraps of paper and stuffed among other cookbooks; many of them are stained and spattered with decade-old ingredients; all of them are beloved and, thus, annotated with ample markings and "lab notes" from years and years of experimental implementation. To me, all of them are treasures and worthy of including and sharing. In future editions, we hope to include savory meal or snack items (for now we have listed them in the "sideboard" as suggested items to prepare throughout the season). I hope by sharing them here now, they will continue to be enjoyed and improved upon. I have loved them all!

BOURBON BALLS
1950s version

2 tbsp. cocoa
1 cup extra fine powdered sugar
More than ¼ cup bourbon
2 tbsp. light corn syrup
2 ½ cups crushed vanilla wafers,
 blended in food processor 15 at a time for
 6 seconds
1 cup bourbonized pecan meat
 i.e. finely-chopped nuts

Sift together the cocoa and the sugar, then stir the bourbon and corn syrup on. Mix together thoroughly the vanilla wafers and the pecans. Roll into balls and dredge with a additional powdered sugar and cocoa.

BOURBON BALLS
Joy, 1964

½ lb. butter
4 oz. condensed milk
Pinch of cream of tartar
1 tsp. salt
3 boxes confectioner's sugar
5 tbsp. bourbon or perhaps a jigger more
2 cups chopped nuts preferably Georgia
 pecan

Have butter at room temperature. Add condensed milk, cream of tartar, and salt. Add 2 boxes of confectioner's sugar and mix well. Add the bourbon! (and sip on a little while you dance around the kitchen in a merry jig.) Add in the nuts. Roll into small balls about the size of a large marble. Put sugar on hands to roll the balls. Place on wax paper. When firm, dip into 8 oz. semi-sweet chocolates.

BRANDY SNAPS
Joy, 1964

½ cup butter
½ cup sugar -or- ¼ cup sugar plus ¼ cup paced maple sugar
⅓ cup dark molasses
¼ tsp. powdered ginger
½ tsp. cinnamon
½ tsp. grated lemon rind -or- orange zest
1 cup King Arthur's all-purpose flour
2 tsp. brandy

Preheat oven to 300. Stir everything but the flour and the brandy over low heat, then add the flour and the brandy. Roll into ¾" balls, then bake on an ungreased baking sheet for about 12 minutes. Remove cookies about a minute from the pan with a spatula then roll over a wooden spoon handle to create batons (may fill with chocolate or such, to preference). Store in a tightly covered tin.

CATHEDRAL PANETTONE
Milan

Panettone pan 7 ½ " in diameter, straight sides 4" high
2 packages active dry yeast
½ cup warm (110) water
⅓ cup granulated sugar
¼ cup warm (110) milk
½ tsp. salt
¼ tsp. freshly-grated nutmeg
⅔ cup butter, softened
2 tsp. freshly-grated orange zest
1 tsp. vanilla extract
3 ¼ cups flour sifted before measuring
2 eggs
2 egg yolks
¼ cup Marsala wine
½ cup golden raisins
⅓ cup slivered candied cherries
⅓ cup slivered diced mixed candied fruits
¼ cup slivered almonds -or- pine nuts
4 - 7 oz. marzipan, finely-chopped to preference
confectioner's sugar

Sprinkle yeast over warm water in large bowl of electric mixer; add 1 teaspoon of the sugar. Let stand until yeast is soft (about 5 minutes). Add remaining sugar, warm milk, salt, nutmeg, butter, orange zest, and vanilla. Add 2 cups of the sifted-flour; mix to blend, the beat until smooth and elastic (about 5 minutes). Beat in the eggs and egg yolks, one at a time. Gradually beat in the remaining 1 ¾ cups [sifted] flour; when it has been added, beat at medium speed until batter is elastic (about 3 minutes).

Transfer batter to a well-greased bowl Cover and let rise in a warm place until bubbly (about 1 hour). While batter s rising, pour Marsala over raisins in a small bowl; set aside to plumpen.

Stir batter down; then gently stir in the raisin mixture, cherries, candied fruits and pine nuts/ almonds, and chopped marzipan until well-distributed. Spread batter in a well-greased, lightly-floured panettone pan. Let rise until doubled (about 30-45 minutes).

Preheat oven to 325°F. Bake until bread is well-browned and a skewer inserted into the center comes out clean 9about 1 - 1 ½ hours). Let stand in pan on wire rack to cool (about 15 minutes), then remove pan and transfer to rack to cool (rounded side up). Dust with confectioners' sugar while warm. Excellent served with coffee -or- champagne!

"CHRISTMAS IN MY MOUTH"
Irene & Peter Harrower

1⅓ cups sugar *less if using Amaretto*
⅔ cup water
2 small navel oranges
2 cups fresh -or- frozen cranberries
   8 oz; thawed if frozen
⅔ tsp. ground cinnamon
freshly-grated nutmeg to preference
⅔ tsp. ground cloves
4 tbsp. minced crystallized ginger
3 tbsp. Amaretto to taste

Bring sugar and water to a boil in a 1 ½ qt. heavy saucepan, stirring until sugar is dissolved. Reduce heat and simmer syrup, without stirring, washing down any sugar crystals on side of pan with a pastry brush dipped in cold water, 5 minutes.

While syrup simmers, cut oranges including pith and peel, into 1-inch pieces, discarding any seeds, and combine with cranberries, cinnamon, and cloves in a food processor.

Add sugar syrup and pulse until fruit is finely chopped. Transfer relish to a bowl and stir in ginger. Chill, covered, 1 day to deepen and develop flavors.

CHRISTMAS PUDDING I.E. FIGGY PUDDING
Marguerite Patten

English 1963

4 oz. flour
2 oz. breadcrumbs
2 eggs
1 tsp. mixed spice
1 level tsp. cinnamon
1 level tsp. freshly-ground nutmeg
4 oz. shredded suet
4 oz. brown sugar
4 oz. grated apple
1 grated carrot, peeled
4 oz. mixed candied peel
4 oz. chopped blanched almonds
¼ pint ale, beer, stout, -or- milk
4 oz. currants
8 oz. raisins
4 oz. sultanas
2 oz. chopped prunes -or- apricots
½ fresh-juiced lemon w/grated rind
½ orange, grated rind
1 tbsp. golden syrup -or- black treacle

It is easier to make breadcrumbs if the bread is firm, but by no account over-stale or nearing "moldy." A good cooking apple gives the best flavour in the pudding. The ale (or beer..) does not prove too strong a flavour to the pudding, but gives a richness to the pudding. Mix all ingredients, together, stir well and leave overnight if possible. Place in 2 smaller basins and cover well with cloth. Steam or boil for 6-8 hours. Cool; remove wet coverings. When cold put on dry covers. Steam for 2 hours on Christmas Day.

THE MOST PROPER CAKE FOR A CHRISTMAS BIRTHDAY

(WITH BONUS INSTRUCTIONS FOR JOVIAL SEASONAL CELEBRATIONS)

BIRTHDAY CAKE

Alice Waters

- 6 eggs *room temperature*
- 1 ½ cups milk
- 4 ½ cups King Arthur cake flour, *well-sifted*
- 6 tsp. baking powder *fresh within 6 months of purchase*
- ¾ tsp. salt *use only ⅝ tsp. if using salted butter*
- 1 ½ cups (*3 sticks*) butter *softened at least 30 minutes at room temperature*
- 3 cups fine-grain sugar
- 1 ½ tsp. vanilla extract

Preheat oven to 350. Butter the 3 9" round cake pans and line the bottom of each with parchment paper. Butter the paper and lightly, but thoroughly, dust the pans with flour, tapping out the excess. Separate (the yolks from the whites) of the eggs, in small bowls. In a larger bowl combine the dry ingredients (well-sifted and exact measurements of flour, baking soda, salt). In another bowl, beat the butter until light and fluffy, then cream with the sugar together until light and fluffy. Beat in the egg yolks, one at a time, then add the vanilla extract. When well mixed, add the flour mixture and the milk, alternatively, starting and ending with ⅓ of the flour. Stir just until the flour is incorporated. In another bowl, whisk the egg whites to soft peaks. Stir one third of the egg whites into the batter, then gently fold in the rest. Pour the batter into the prepared cake pans and bake in the center of the oven until a toothpick inserted into the center comes out clean, about 30-40 minutes (do not disturb the cake for at least the first 15-20 minutes). Let it cool. Remove from pans, invert onto cooling racks, add icing, decorate, add 2018 candles, and sing "Happy Birthday!" as everyone with Christmas in their hearts (or chosen delegate), blows out the candles and makes a Christmas Birthday wish!

A FOND ACKNOWLEDGEMENT AND MEMORY OF:

MARIAN EXALL who contributed the authentic British recipes (English, 1963). The mother of a dear best friend, who welcomed me into their home in Bellingham, when I was far away from my own in Atlanta, and invigorated my imagination with the Spirit of Christmas.

ELVEN BREAD
adapted from Alice Waters

(aka Anise-Almond Biscotti)

1 ½ cup whole almonds
2 ¼ cups unbleached all-purpose King Arthur's flour *well-sifted before measuring*
1 tsp. baking powder
2 tsp. aniseed
1 ½ tsp. fennel seeds
a few coriander seeds *tapped with a mortar and pestle*
3 eggs *at room temperature at least 30 minutes prior*
1 cup sugar
½ tsp. lemon zest
½ tsp. almond extract
½ tsp. vanilla extract

Preheat the oven to 350°F. Roughly half the almonds then spread out on a baking sheet to toast in the oven for 5 minutes, stirring every minute or so; let them cool, then coarsely chop. Measure and stir together the dry ingredients (excepting the sugar). In a separate bowl, beat the eggs until uniform then add in the sugar, the extracts, and the lemon zest. Beat until the sugar is dissolving-ish and the mixture forms a delightfully enchanting ribbon. Gently stir in the flour mixture until just incorporated and then doubly-gently stir in the almonds. You don't want to overbeat or the biscotti will be hard and dense.

On a parchment-lined baking sheet, form the dough into two 3"-wide loaves, about 3" apart. Smooth the loaves with damp hands. Bake for 25 minutes or until lightly golden. Remove the loaves from the oven and let cool for about 10 minutes. Lower the oven temperature to 300. Cut the cooled loaves into ½" thick cookes and palce cut-side down on 2 baking sheets. Cook for 10 minutes, turn the cookies over, and cook for another 10 minutes, or until golden brown. May store in a cookie tin for quite some time.

"FATHER TIME" PIE
Joy, 1964

A baked pie shell
½ cup butter *left at room temperature at least 30 minutes prior to creaming*
2 cups packed light brown sugar
4 egg yolks
2 tbsp. all-purpose flour
1 tsp. cinnamon
½ tsp. allspice
1 tsp. freshly-grated nutmeg
1 cup cream
½ cup chopped dates
½ cup raisins
½ cup broken pecan meats.

Preheat the oven to 325°F. Prepare the pie shell {as described above}. Cream the butter and the sugar until light and smooth. Beat in the egg yolks until even lighter and smoother. Mix together the dry ingredients in a separate bowl then add them to the butter, sugar, and egg mixture. Then, slowly stir in cream and the remaining ingredients. When set, bake the pie about 30 minutes. When cool top with Meringue {see below} and bake 10-15 minutes, depending on thickness.

TO MAKE: MERINGUE

2 egg whites
1/4 tsp. cream of tartar
3 tbsp. sugar -or- 4 tbsp. powdered sugar
1/2 tsp. vanilla

Whip the egg whites until light and frothy. Add the cream of tartar. Whip until stiff, but not dry, until they stand in peaks that lean over slightly when the beater is removed. Then beat in the sugar 1/2 teaspoon at a time.

GERMAN MARZIPAN STOLLEN

Joy, 1964

6 cups well-sifted all-purpose flour
1 1/2 - 2 cakes compressed yeast
1 1/2 cups 85-degree water -or- milk
1/2 lb. raisins
1/2 lb. blanched chopped almonds
1/2 cup chopped candied fruits
3/4 cup sugar
1 1/2 cups butter, softened at room temperature
3 eggs
3/4 tsp. salt
3/4 tsp. freshly-grated lemon rind
4 - 7 oz. marzipan, chopped
2 tbsp. brandy -or -rum
Milk -or- **lemon glaze** {see below}

Crumble the yeast into the warm water -or- warm milk for about 10 minutes until dissolved. Add 1 cup of sifted flour. Permit this sponge to rise in a warm place until doubled in bulk. Sprinkle a little of the sifted flour over the fruit. Sift the sugar. And beat the butter until soft, adding the sugar gradually. Blend until light and

cream, then (one at a time) beat in the eggs; add in the salt, lemon, and spirits. Add the yeast mixture (e.g. "sponge") and the remaining flour. Knead the dough until it is smooth and elastic. Permit it to rise until it doubles in bulk. Toss it onto a floured board. Add fruits, nuts, and marzipan. Divide into 2 loaves then place them into greased-and-floured non-sticking pans. Brush their tops with sufficient melted butter to cover. Cover with a clean kitchen towel. Let the loaves rise,, until again they are almost doubled in bulk (third time!). Preheat the oven to 350°F. Bake the loaves for about 45 minutes. When cool, brush with milk or a lemon glaze.

TO MAKE: LEMON GLAZE

1 1/4 cup confectioners' sugar
1/4 cup fresh-squeezed lemon, orange, lime -or- other citrus juice
1 tsp. vanilla

Mix or blend until smooth.

(OLD FASHIONED) GINGER COOKIES

3/4 c. sugar
1/2 c. spry* also known as "shortening"
1/4 tsp. salt
1 egg
1 cup blackstrap molasses
1 tsp. cinnamon
1 tsp. cloves
2 tsp. ginger or more
2 1/2 cups flour
1 1/2 tsp. baking soda
some tiny cut-up crystallized ginger
freshly-grated nutmeg to taste about 1 tsp

Mix all the dry ingredients, upon sifting the flour.

In a separate bowl, mix spry, molasses, sugar (until of one color and texture), then beat in egg. Make into small ball that fits into palm of hand (slightly smaller than a golf ball). Roll into sugar. Press with lovely-etched glass.

Grease cookie sheet with butter, bake 350°F for 10 minutes.

MINCE PIES
Marguerite Patten

TO MAKE: THE MINCEMEAT
(or use "Cross and Blackwell" available for purchase in a jar)

4 oz. shredded suet
4 oz. grated apples
1 lb. mixed dried fruit
4 oz. sugar *preferably brown*
4 oz. blanched and well-dried almonds
4 oz. mixed peel
1 large lemon, finely grated rind and juice, thereof
1 tsp. mixed spice
½ tsp. cinnamon
½ tsp. nutmeg
4 tbsp. brandy *-or-* whisky *-or-* rum

It is absolutely essential to make sure the fruit is perfectly dry before making mincemeat. If you have washed it let it dry for at least 24 hours prior, preferably 48 hours before using. A good cooking apple should be used. Make certain your jars are clean and very dry.

Mix all ingredients together. Put into dry jam jars and cover thoroughly. Use both wax circles and a cellophane or paper top. Store in a cool, dry place.

TO MAKE: SHORT CRUST PASTRY

8 oz. plain *-or-* self-rising flour
3 ½ oz. whipped-up cooking fat
½ level tsp. salt
2-3 tbsp. cold water

Rubbed whipped-up cooking fat into the sieved flour and salt, until the mixture looks like fine breadcrumbs. Rub quickly and lightly and lift the mixture up all the time to get as much cool air as possible. Add freshly drawn cold (-or- iced) water, using tablespoon to be accurate; sprinkle evenly over the mixture. Take a palette knife or any round-bladed kitchen knife and mix together lightly, cutting through and pressing together. A knife is used to keep the pastry cool. Put down the knife and quickly bind together the mixture into a smooth dough with the hand (holding the bowl with the other hand), and leaving the bowl clean of all dough particles. Place the dough on a LIGHTLY floured board or table top and remove all cracks by kneading lightly. Flour the rolling pin lightly, and using short sharp strokes, roll the pastry to whatever shape is required. Roll in one direction only, and turn the pastry as necessary, taking care not to stretch it. Bake as directed later in this recipe.

TO MAKE: THE PIES

8 oz. of short crust pastry
Approximately 6-8 oz. of mincemeat

Roll out the pastry (if you haven't already done so as described above). Cut into rounds for the base of the pies, using a cutter a little larger than the pastry tins. Press the rounds of pastry into each tin. This quantity of pastry should make 12 pies. Put on a spoonful of mincemeat (you should not be too generous or this boils out in cooking and makes the tarts sticky). Cut out 12 rounds for the lids, these need to be a little bit smaller than the previous ones. Press the edges together. Make a slit on top with scissors or a sharp knife. Bake for 20-25 minutes just above the centre of a hot oven (450°F, Gas Mark 7), if necessary reducing the heat after 15 minutes.

> "Heaped up on the floor, to form a kind of throne, were turkeys, geese, game, poultry, brawn, great joints of meat, sucking pigs, long wreaths of sausages, mince-pies, plum-puddings, barrels of oysters, red-hot chestnuts, cherry-cheeked apples, juicy oranges, luscious pears, immense twelfth-cakes, and seething bowl of punch, that made the chamber dim with their delicious steam."
>
> – CHARLES DICKENS,
> A CHRISTMAS CAROL,
> 1843

MINCEMEAT PIES
Joy, 1964

9 quarts apples, *peeled and sliced*
4 lbs. lean, chopped beef *-or-* ox heart
2 lbs. chopped beef suet
3 lbs. sugar
2 quarts cider
4 lbs. seeded raisins
3 lbs. currants
1 ½ lbs. chopped citron
½ lb. dried, chopped, candied orange peel
½ lb. dried, chopped, candied lemon peel
Juice and rind of one lemon
1 tbsp. cinnamon
1 tbsp. mace
1 tbsp. cloves
1 tsp. salt
1 tsp. pepper
2 whole freshly-grated nutmegs
1 gallon sour cherries *with their juices*
2 lbs. broken nut meat *pecans, walnuts,*

etc.
1 tsp. powdered coriander seed

Prepare the apples, then combine with all the other ingredients in a large pot. Cook slowly for 2 hours, stirring frequently. Distribute into jars, seal and allow to sit for at least 2 weeks (in the refrigerator). Then, fashion into pies seasoning with about 4 tablespoons of brandy. Cover the pie with the upper crust and bake at 450°F for about 30 minutes.

An alternative is to assemble into a pie crust round in an ovenproof dish using hot (warmed in saucepan) mincemeat, then pour ⅓ cup warmed brandy over the mincemeat to ignite at the table.

PLUM PUDDING
Gary Carl Furin, 1974

To make 4 1-quart puddings -or- 2 2-quart puddings

1 ½ cups dried currants
2 cups seedless raisins
2 cups white raisins
¾ cup finely chopped candied mixed fruit peel
¾ cup finely chopped candied cherries
1 cup blanched slivered almonds
1 medium-sized tart cooking apple, *peeled, quartered, cored, and coarsely chopped*
1 small carrot, *scraped and coarsely chopped*
2 tbsp. finely grated orange peel
2 tsp. finely grated lemon peel
½ pound finely chopped beef [kidney] suet
2 cups all-purpose flour
4 cups fresh soft crumbs, *made from homemade-type white bread, pulverized in a blender -or- shredded with a fork*

1 cup dark-brown sugar
1 tsp. ground allspice
1 tsp. salt
6 eggs
1 cup brandy
  cup fresh orange juice
  cup fresh lemon juice
½ cup brandy, for flaming *optional*

In a large deep bowl, combine currants, seedless raisins, white raisins, candied fruit peel, cherries, almonds, apple, carrot, orange and lemon peel, and beef suet, tossing them about with a spoon or your hands until well mixed. Stir in flour, bread crumbs, brown sugar, allspice, and salt.

In a separate bowl, beat the eggs until frothy. Stir in the 1 cup of brandy, the orange and lemon juice, and pour this mixture over the fruit mixture. Knead vigorously with both hands, then beat with a wooden spoon until all the ingredients are blended. Drape a dampened kitchen towel over the bowl and refrigerate for at least 12 hours.

(takes 2 - 2 ½ hrs. to complete the above steps)

Grease and flour inside of the molds 1st. Remember to tap flour.

Spoon the mixture into 4 1-quart English pudding basins or plain molds, filling them to within 2 inches of their tops. Cover each mold with a strip of buttered foil, turning the edges down and pressing the foil tightly around the sides to secure it. Drape a dampened kitchen towel over each mold and tie it in place around the sides with a long piece of kitchen cord. Bring two opposite corners of the towel up to the top and knot them in the center of the mold; then bring up the remaining two corners and knot them similarly.

Place the molds in a large pot and pour in enough boiling water to come about ¾ of the way up their sides. Bring the water to a boil over high heat, cover the pot tightly, reduce the heat to its lowest point and steam the puddings for 8 hours. As the water in the steamer boils away replenish it with additional boiling water.

When the puddings are done, remove them from the water and let them cool to room temperature. Then remove the towels and foil and re-cover the molds tightly with fresh foil. Refrigerate the puddings for at least 3 weeks before serving. Plum puddings may be kept up to a year in the refrigerator or other cool place; traditionally, they were often made a year in advance.

To serve, place the mold in a pot and pour in enough boiling water to come about ¾ of the way up the sides of the mold. Bring to a boil over high heat, cover the pot, reduce the heat to low and steam for 2-hours. Run a knife around the inside edges of the mold and place an inverted serving plate over it. Grasping the mold and plate firmly together, turn them over. The pudding should slide out easily

If you would like to set the pudding aflame before you serve it warm the ½* cup of brandy in a small saucepan over low heat, ignite it with a match and pour it over the pudding.

* a little much. A ⅓ or a ¼ ought to do fine

BRANDY BUTTER
To make about ¾ cup

4 tbsp. unsalted butter, softened! *Be quite sure the butter's soft 1st from sitting out; curdles otherwise*
½ cup superfine sugar *i.e. confectioner's*
3 tbsp. brandy

½ tsp. vanilla extract

Combine the butter, sugar, brandy and vanilla in a bowl, and beat with an electric beater until the mixture is smooth and well blended. (Whether "by hand" or "with an electric beater," cream the butter by beating and mashing it against the sides of the mixing bowl until it is light and fluffy. Beat in the sugar, a few tablespoons at a time, and continue beating until the mixture is very white and frothy. Beat in the brandy and vanilla). Refrigerate at least 4 hours, or until firm. Brandy butter is traditionally served with plum pudding, and may be sprinkled with ground nutmeg before serving.

-AND-OR-

CUMBERLAND RUM BUTTER
To make about ¾ cup

4 tbsp. unsalted butter, softened!
½ cup light-brown sugar, rubbed
   through a sieve
¼ cup light rum
⅛ tsp. ground nutmeg

Combine the butter, sugar, rum and nutmeg in a bowl and beat with an electric beater until the mixture is smooth and well blended. (Whether "by hand" or "with an electric beater," cream the butter by beating and mashing it against the sides of the mixing bowl until it is light and fluffy. Beat in the sugar, a few tablespoons at a time, and then the rum and nutmeg). Refrigerate at least 4 hours, or until firm. Brandy butter is traditionally served with plum pudding.

PUMPKIN PIE
Joy, 1964

A baked pie shell
1 ½ cups cooked pumpkin -or- local
   seasonal squash
1 ½ cups rich cream
6 tbsp. brown sugar
2 tbsp. white sugar
½ tsp. salt
1 tsp. cinnamon
½ tsp. ginger
⅛ tsp. cloves
½ cup molasses
3 eggs
1 cup molasses
1 tsp. vanilla -or- 1 tbsp. rum
¾ cup black walnut meats
whipped cream

Prepare for a 9" pie. Mix the pumpkin, cream, sugar, salt, spices, molasses, and eggs in the top of a double boiler until thick (over the hot water, not in it). Allow to cool, then add the vanilla / rum and the walnut meats (optional). Pour the mixture into the baked pie shell, then serve with house-made whipped cream.

PECAN PIE
Joy, 1964

An unfilled pie shell
¼ - ⅓ cup room-temperature butter
   allow to sit out for at least 30 minutes prior
1 cup firmly packed brown sugar
4 eggs
1 cup molasses
1-2 cups broken Georgia pecans
1 tsp. vanilla
1 tbsp. rum
½ tsp. salt

Preheat the oven to 450°F. Bake the pie-shell partially (about 5-7 minutes), and allow to cool while you prepare the filling. Lower the temperature to 350°F.

Cream the butter and the sugar. Beat in the eggs one at a time until well-incorporated and light. Then, stir in the remaining ingredients. Fill the shell. Bake the pie for about 30 minutes at 350°F or until a knife inserted into the center comes out clean. Serve warm or cold. Ideally with a digestif cocktail, and perhaps a dollop of vanilla ice-cream.

PFEFFERNUSSE
Joy, 1964

1/2 cup butter
1/2 cup sugar
2 well-beaten eggs
1 cup sifted King Arthur's all-purpose flour
1/4 tsp. each salt and soda
1/2 tsp. each freshly-ground black pepper, nutmeg, cloves, and allspice
1 tsp. cinnamon
1/8 tsp. freshly-ground cardamom
   use a mortar and pestle
1-3 drops oil of anise -or- 1/4 cups ground blanched almonds
1 1/2 tbsp. freshly-grated lemon peel
1/4 cup chopped citron

Preheat oven to 350°F. Cream together the butter, sugar, and well-beaten eggs. In a separate bowl, sift the rest of the ingredients together, then add them to the butter, sugar, eggs bowl. Form into palm-size balls (slightly smaller than golf balls), space cookies about 2 inches apart then bake 10-12 minutes. Store tightly covered in a Christmas cookie tin.

PISTACHIO ICE CREAM
Joy, 1964

4 oz. pistachio nuts *shell them*
A few drops of rose water
1/4 cup sugar
1/4 cup cream

1/2 tsp. almond extract
A hint of all-natural green food coloring
1 cup cream
3/4 cup sugar
1/8 tsp. salt
2 cups whipping cream
1 cup cream

Blanch the pistachios. In a bowl mix 1/4 cup sugar, 1/4 cup cream, the vanilla and almond extracts, and greenness (do not yet add the pistaches); stir until the sugar is dissolved, then heat, without bringing to a boil, the additional 1 cup of cream. Stir in the additional 3/4 cup sugar and the salt. Once fully dissolved, remove from heat and chill the mixture. Add the pistachios and the whipping cream and additional 1 cup of cream. Churn in an ice-cream maker or other preferred method until ready.

RICH CHRISTMAS CAKE
Marguerite Patten

12 oz. plain flour
3/4 oz. level tsp. salt
1 1/2 level tsp. cinnamon
1 1/2 rounded tsp. mixed spice
3/4 tsp. freshly-ground nutmeg
1 1/2 pounds seedless raisins
1 1/2 pounds sultanas
18 oz. currants
1 1/2 level tsp. black treacle
5 tbsp. brandy
6 oz. chopped candied peel
6 oz. glazed cherries
6 oz. blanched almonds
12 oz. butter
12 oz. soft brown sugar
8 eggs
2oz. plain chocolate *to darken the cake without flavoring it*

Preheat the oven to Gas Mark 3 (between

325 - 350°F) Sieve together dry ingredients, chop cherries and almonds. In a separate bowl, cream butter and sugar together until light and fluffy, then add the black treacle. Beat the eggs (in, yet another separate bowl), and add to the butter and sugar. Melt the chocolate, cool and fold into mixture with flour, fruit, and brandy. Turn mixture into 2 greased double-lined 9" cake tins. Bake in the center for 1 ½ hrs., then reduce heat to Gas Mark 2 (between 275 - 300) to bake a further 1 ½ - 2 hours. Allow cake to cool before removing from tins. Place in an airtight tin until required. Cover with marzipan and decorate to heart's content.

TO MAKE: MARZIPAN

12 oz. ground almonds
6 oz. castor sugar
6 oz. icing sugar
Several drops almond essence
3 egg yolks to mix

Marzipan should not be over-handled or it becomes oily and sticky. Buy your ground almonds fresh or store in a wax container so they do not spoil. Sieve the icing sugar. It is very hard and and it is easier if you roll this with a rolling pin between 2 sheets of greaseproof paper then rub it through the sieve. Mix all ingredients, adding enough egg yolks to make a firm mixture. Knead thoroughly, but do not overhandle.

To coat the cake, brush away loose crumbs from the cake. Spread the sides of the cake with either egg whites or with sieved apricot jam. Roll out marzipan on a sugared board or table. Measure the circumference and depth of the cake. Cut a strip exactly the length of the circumference plus about ⅛" — and 1" deeper for the depth. Use approximately half or just over half of total amount of marzipan. Cut a round of marzipan the size the top

of the cake. Hold the cake on its side, then just as you were rolling a hoop, roll along the strip of marzipan. If you do this firmly, then the marzipan sticks to the cake. Make sure the extra inch is at the top of the cake. Turn the cake back onto its base again, seal the joint firmly and press down the extra inch on the top. Brush top with egg white or apricot jam and press round of marzipan into position. Tidy sides by rolling a jam jar or rolling pin held upright along the sides of the cake. Roll top to give a neat edge, this makes icing the cake much easier. If you are fairly practiced in handling marzipan you will be able to put the icing on straight away. If however you feel you have had to knead the marzipan a fair amount to make it pliable, it is much better to let it dry out for 48 hours.

SCONES
Alice Waters

2 cups unbleached whole-wheat King Arthur pastry flour -or- all purpose flour
2 ½ tsp. fresh baking powder
½ tsp. salt
¼ cup sugar + 1 ½ tbsp. sugar
1 cup cream
2 tbsp. butter, melted

Preheat the oven to 400°F. Measure and mix together the dry ingredients (excepting the tablespoons of sugar) in a large bowl.* Stir in the cream. Mix until the dough just starts to come together, it will be sticky. Turn it out onto a floured surface and knead briefly, just enough to bring the dough completely together. Pat it into an 8" circle, then brush with the melted butter and sprinkle with the remaining sugar. Cut the circle into 8 wedges (or 8 rounds) and place them 1" apart on a baking sheet lined with parchment paper. Bake for 17 minutes or until golden brown.

IS IT CHRISTMAS YET?

(A NON-COMPREHENSIVE LIST
OF HOLIDAY DATES AND DEFINITIONS)

"12 DAYS OF CHRISTMAS"
(also known as Twelvetide,
Christmastide, or Yuletide)
December 26 – January 6

CHRISTMAS SEASON
Late November to Early January

SATURNALIA
(sometimes known as "The
Golden Days of Christmas)

Ancient Roman festival in
celebration of the god Saturn.

Originally on December 17, but
expanded with festivities through
December 23.

ADVENT
The beginning of the Western
liturgical year; commences on the
fourth Sunday before Christmas.*

WINTER SOLSTICE
The longest night, after
which the days incrementally
become lighter.

*WHAT DATE DOES ADVENT START ON?

As the Catholic Encyclopedia notes, "Advent is a period beginning with the Sunday nearest to the feast of St. Andrew the Apostle (30 November) and embracing four Sundays." That means that the First Sunday of Advent can fall as early as November 27 or as late as December 3.

*to the dry ingredients you may add ½ cup chopped dried fruit (apricots, nectarines, pears) or dried cherries, cranberries, currants, raisins, etc! You may also choose to add the zest of preferred citrus, and/ or other spices and variations to your preferred tastes (savory or sweet) and that of your Elevenses or afternoon tea-time guests.'

SPICED CARROT CAKE
de la Foret, the Grit

TO MAKE: THE CAKE

6 tbsp. coconut flour, sifted
1 tbsp. ground cinnamon
1 tsp. freshly-grated nutmeg
1 tsp. powdered-ginger
½ tsp. ground cloves
½ tsp. baking soda
½ tsp. salt
5 eggs
1 tbsp. pure vanilla extract
½ cup Lamb Sugarworks Dark
  Robust maple syrup
½ cup coconut oil, melted
3 raw carrots, peeled and grated
½ cup raisins

Preheat the oven to 325°F. In a small bowl, mix the coconut flour, spices, baking soda, and salt. In a large mixing bowl, beat the eggs, vanilla, maple syrup and melted coconut oil. Add the dry ingredients to large bowl and mix well. Stir in the carrots and raisins. Grease a 9x9" cake pan with coconut oil, pour the batter into the pan, then bake for 30 minutes. Test the center with a toothpick, when it comes out clean, the cake is done. Remove the cake from the oven and allow to cool while you make the frosting.

TO MAKE: THE FROSTING:

8 oz. cream cheese, softened
½ cup butter, softened at room
  temperature

¼ cup Lamb Sugarworks maple syrup
1 tbsp. pure vanilla extract
1 tbsp. freshly-grated ginger
1 cup chopped walnuts, for garnish

Cream together the cream cheese and the butter. Mix in the maple syrup and vanilla extract. Stir in the freshly-grated ginger. Once the cake has cooled, frost it with the buttercream frosting. Garnish with chopped walnuts and serve.

> "Blessed is the season which engages the whole world in a conspiracy of love."
>
> – HAMILTON WRIGHT MABIE

SUE SUE'S CHRISTMAS COOKIES
Suzanne Windjue Walter

⅔ cup shortening
¾ cup granulated organic sugar
1 tsp. vanilla
1 organic pasture-raised egg
2 tsps. milk
2 cups sifted organic flour
1 ½ tsp. baking powder
¼ tsp. salt

TO MAKE: THE ICING

¾ box organic powdered sugar
1 tsp. vanilla
2 tbsp organic grass-fed butter
2 tbsp. milk

Thoroughly cream shortening, sugar, and vanilla. Add egg, beat until light and fluffy. Stir in milk. In a separate bowl, sift together dry ingredients; then blend into creamed mixture. Divide dough in half. Chill one hour.

Place ball between two sheets of waxed paper. Roll to about ¼" thickness. Cut into shapes (discs).

Bake at 375°F for about 6-8 minutes.

Cool slightly and remove from cookie sheets. Decorate with icing and festive cheer.

TQM'S GINGER SCONES

Conrad Bladey's Irish Teatime Companion

2 cups all-purpose flour *plus additional flour for working the dough*
¼ cup granulated fair-trade sugar *plus additional for dusting the tops*
2 teaspoons baking powder
1/8 teaspoon salt
⅓ cups grass-fed unsalted butter, chilled *plus additional for the baking sheet*
½ cup heavy (whipping) cream
1 large egg
1 ½ teaspoons vanilla extract

OPTIONAL INGREDIENTS:

½ cup low-sugar, very spicy crystal-ized ginger
1 egg mixed with 1 teaspoon water for glaze

Preheat the oven to 425°F. Lightly butter a baking sheet.

In a large bowl, stir together the flour, sugar, baking powder and salt. Cut the butter in ½ inch cubes and add to the flour mixture. With a pastry blender or 2 knives in scissor-fashion, cut in the butter until the mixture resembles coarse crumbs. In a small bowl, stir together the cream, 1 egg, and vanilla. Add the cream mixture to the flour mixture and stir until just combined. Stir in the crystalized ginger and other optional ingredients.

With lightly-floured hands, pat the dough to a ½ inch thickness on a lightly-floured cutting board. Using a floured 2 ½-inch diameter round biscuit cutter or a glass, cut out round from the dough and place them on the prepared baking sheet. Gather the scraps together and repeat until all the dough is used.

Lightly brush the tops of the scones with the egg mixture, if desired. Bake until lightly browned, 13-15 minutes. Remove the baking sheet to a wire rack and cool for 5 minutes. Serve either barely warm or cool.

"Heap on more wood!-the wind is chill
But let it whistle as it will,
We'll keep our Christmas merry still."

- SIR WALTER SCOTT

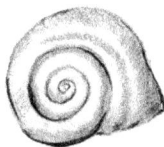

SIDEBOARD

ADDITIONAL RECIPES TO CONSIDER:

BORSCHT
(DE LA FORET, GARY CARL FURIN)

APPLES (SWEET ONIONS,
KIELBASA SAUSAGE,
SAUERKRAUT)

GOOSE

ROAST STUFFED TURKEY

DRESSING

RED CABBAGE WITH BACON

OXFORDSHIRE FISH PIE

FRENCH BREAD

ESCARGOT

CHAMPAGNE TOASTS FOR
CHRISTMAS AND NEW YEAR'S

NEW YEAR'S AT MIDNIGHT
DRINKING CHOCOLATE

BLACK-EYED PEAS, HOG JOWLS,
AND COLLARD GREENS, NEW
YEAR'S DAY

PULLED MINTS

PEPPERMINT BARK

LAVENDER AND ORANGE
CUSTARD

CARDAMOM AND CHOCOLATE
MOUSSE CAKE

CHOCOLATE STRAWBERRY
PUDDING

TURKISH DELIGHT

ASTRAGALUS BONE BROTH

ROASTED POTATOES WITH
PARSLEY

ROASTED ROOT VEGETABLES
WITH FENNEL

ROSEMARY LAMB

SAGE CHICKEN

SQUASH SOUP WITH MUSTARD
SEEDS

BRUSSELS SPROUTS

MULLIGATAWNY SOUP

OYSTERS ROCKEFELLER

ROSEMARY LAMB

CATHERINE STANDBACK'S
HOUSE-MADE APPLESAUCE

ALPINE RD.'S SWEET AND SPICY
PECANS

IN CONCLUSION

APPENDIX:
ACKNOWLEDGMENTS, ATTRIBUTIONS, AND ADDITIONAL RESOURCES

Listed below are the resources I used to stand on the shoulders of giants in the construction of this compendium. They are listed in the order in which I happened to be inspired in the "researching for" and "writing of" this little book, which I thought a rather interesting evolution, and so decided to leave it as such.

BOOKS

The "bolded" words reflect from which works I directly referenced, and thus noted above throughout the cocktail section. Although many of the recipes included in this Christmas Cocktail Book are time-honored traditions, I wanted to nod towards the author/ mixologists from which I gleaned my original awareness and insight. This is not to say that this "author" was in fact the originator of this recipe, but it is this noted author through which I first discovered the foundational recipe from which my work rises. Perhaps, an edition in the near future might include more origin-stories, but this first edition is a humble little book, with humble origins, and thus providing ample room to mature and grow.

*The Waldorf Astoria Bar Book
by Frank Caiafa, 2016

The Old Waldorf-Astoria Bar book
by Albert Stevens Crockett, 1934

* The PDT Cocktail Book: The Complete Bartender's Guide from the Celebrated Speakeasy
by Jim Meehan, 2011

Meehan's Bartender Manual
by Jim Meehan

* Imbibe!: From Absinthe Cocktail to Whiskey Smash, a Salute in Stories and Drinks to "Professor" Jerry Thomas, Pioneer of the American Bar
by David Wondrich, 2008

Punch: The Delights (and Dangers) of the Flowing Bowl
by David Wondrich

Liquid Intelligence:

The Art and Science of the Perfect Cocktail
by Dave Arnold, 2015

Death & Co.:
Modern Classic Cocktails
by Alex Day, 2015

James Beard Foundation

John T. Edge

* The Bitter Southerner

The Drunken Botanist: The Plants that Create the World's Great Drinks
by Amy Stewart, 2013

The Wildcrafted Cocktail:
Make your Own Foraged Syrups, Bitters, Infusions, and Garnishes
by Ellen Zachos, 2017

DIY Bitters: Reviving the Forgotten Flavor, A Guide to Making your own Bitters for Bartenders, Cocktail

Enthusiasts, and Herbalists
by Guido Mase and Jovial King, 2016

Bitters: A Spirited History of a
Classic Cure-All with Cocktails,
Recipes, and Formulas
by Brad Thomas Parsons, 2011

Alchemy of Herbs:
Transform Everyday Ingredients into
Foods & Remedies that Heal
by Rosalee De La Foret, 2017

Shrubs: An Old-Fashioned
Drink for Modern Times
by Michael Dietsch, 2016

Cocktails: How to Mix Them
by Robert Vermeire, 1922

Bottoms Up:
52 Cock-Tail Spins for High Flyers
by Two Knights and a Maid, assisted by
John Walker and the Haig Bros, 1928

Official Mixer's Manual
by Patrick Gavin Duffy, 1934

Cafe Royal Cocktail Book
by W.J. Tarling, 1937

The Gentleman's Companion
by Charles Baker, 1939

* The Savoy Cocktail Book
by Harry Craddock, 1930

* Bartenders Guide
by Jerry Thomas, 1862

*** Old Mr. Boston's deLuxe
Official Bartender's Guide**

* Wild Drinks and Cocktails:
Handcrafted Squushes, Shrubs,
Switchels, Tonics, and Infusions
by Emily Han, 2015

Cocktail Chemistry Lab
cocktailchemistrylab.com

*The Art of Simple Food
by Alice Waters, 2007

The Flowing Bowl:
When and What to Drink
by William Schmidt, 1891

The Fine Art of Mixing Drinks
by David A. Embury, 1948

Wild Fermentation:
The Flavor, Nutrition, and Craft
of Live-Culture Foods
by Sandor Katz, 2003

Good Life Revival
by Sam Sycamore, 2017

Make Mead Like a Viking
by Jereme Zimmerman, 2015

*** Marguerite Patton's
Step-by-Step Cookery**
by Paul Hamlyn, London 1963

*** The Hawk and the Owl, Private
Drinking House**

Prohibition in Atlanta: Temperance,
Tiger Kings, and White Lightning
by Ron Smith and Mary O. Boyle, 2015

The Emerald Tablet: Alchemy for
Personal Transformation
by Dennis William Hauck, 1999

Full Moon Feast: Food and
the Hunger for Connection
by Jessica Prentice, 2006

A Christmas Carol
by Charles Dickens, 1843

To order additional copies of this title, visit:
https://tinyurl.com/y3b2nj4q

ESTABLISHMENTS

Finally, I have also included a list of influential artisan bars and other providers aligned with the values of this book from which I, along with dear friends, performed ample "market research" with the hopes that you will do similarly.

ATLANTA, GA

18.21 Bitters

Bantam Pub

Church

Concrete Jungle

Edgar's Proofs and Provisions

Empire State South

The Fabulous Fox Theatre

Green's Package Store

Holman and Finch

JCT.

Ladybird

The Lawrence

The Miracle Pop-Up Bar

The Mercury

Miller Union

Octane

Old 4th Ward Distillery

Ormsby's

Paper Crane Lounge

PDH.

The Pinewood

The Polaris

Ration & Dram

Red Phone Booth

Seven Lamps

The Sound Table

Staplehouse

Tower Package Store

Ticonderoga Club

Venkman's

Westside Provisions

the Wrecking Bar

Your Dekalb Farmers' Market

DECATUR, GA

Kimball House

LOUISVILLE, KY

Seelbach Hotel

HOOD RIVER, OR

Clear Creek Distillery

PORTLAND, OR

Albina Press

Backyard Social

Beaker and Flask
(former establishment of drinkware inspiration)

Bit House Saloon

Bollywood Theatre

Clyde Common

Coava Coffee Roasters

The Green Room

Interurban

La Moule

Multnomah Whisky
Library

Pok Pok

The Secret Society

Sidecar 11

Tao of Tea

Wildwood
(former esteemed
predecessor for Portland
restaurateurs)

RICHMOND, VA

The Roosevelt

BAINBRIDGE, WA

Battle Point Distillery

SEATTLE, WA

The Collective

Marjorie

"PEACE AND PLENTY FOR MANY A CHRISTMAS TO COME."

- IRISH BLESSING

INDEX

NOTABLE SIDEBAR ITEMS

RECIPES

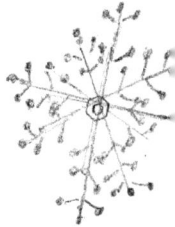

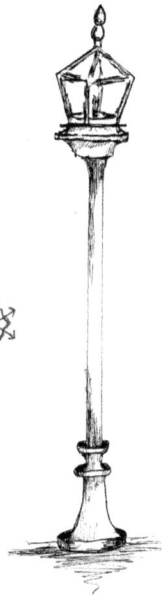

NOTES

....

....

....

....

....

....

....

....

....

....

....

....

....

....

....

....

....

....

....

....

....

....

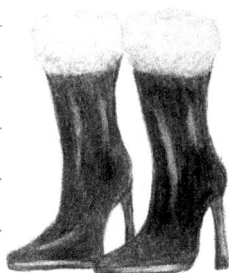

....

....

....

....

....

www.ingramcontent.com/pod-product-compliance
Lightning Source LLC
Chambersburg PA
CBHW051843090426
42736CB00011B/1927